SILVERED WINGS

SILVERED WINGS

by

Air Vice-Marshal Sir John Severne
KCVO OBE AFC DL

Foreword by

HRH The Duke of Edinburgh KG KT

Pen & Sword
AVIATION

First published in Great Britain in 2007 by
Pen & Sword Military
an imprint of
Pen & Sword Books Ltd
47 Church Street
Barnsley
South Yorkshire
S70 2AS

Copyright © John Severne 2007

ISBN: 978-1-84415-559-0

A CIP catalogue record for this book is
available from the British Library.

Typeset in 11/13pt Ehrhardt by Concept, Huddersfield
Printed and bound in England by Biddles Ltd

Pen & Sword Books Ltd incorporates the imprints of Pen & Sword Aviation,
Pen & Sword Maritime, Pen & Sword Military, Wharncliffe Local History,
Pen & Sword Select, Pen and Sword Military Classics and Leo Cooper.

For a complete list of Pen & Sword titles please contact
Pen & Sword Books Limited
47 Church Street, Barnsley, South Yorkshire, S70 2AS, England
E-mail: enquiries@pen-and-sword.co.uk
Website: www.pen-and-sword.co.uk

Contents

For my family

Foreword

BUCKINGHAM PALACE.

    John Severne is a very lucky fellow. There are not many people who have a single-minded ambition about what they want to do with their lives; who manage to realise that ambition, and then turn out to have a real talent for it. As this book makes abundantly clear, flying was his consuming passion, and it gave him years of satisfaction, a career filled with challenges overcome, and the comradeship of a very wide circle of service and other friends.

    I was very fortunate to get him as my Equerry, and later to have him as Captain of the Queen's Flight. Having learned to fly both fixed and rotary wing aircraft, and having the obligation to travel a great deal both in this country and abroad, I relished every opportunity to fly myself. This was made much easier with the help of someone who was only too willing to aid and abet me. I have many reasons to be grateful to him, and I hope his book will give pleasure and interest to aviators and aviation enthusiasts of all kinds.

Preface

Recently I was discussing the King's Cup Air Race with a retired aeronautical engineering friend when he said, 'You must have led a very interesting life', and when I thought about it I had to agree. He said I should write a book and several people in the past have suggested that, but I had not previously considered it would be worth attempting because I have never kept a diary and I doubted that I had anything worth writing about that would interest others. However, now that I am well and truly retired, I have had time to reflect on all those happy memories which now keep flooding back and so I decided I would try to share with others the joy of flying which I have experienced, and to discuss some of the interesting appointments I have had during my RAF career.

Acknowledgements

My grateful thanks go to Graham Pitchfork for pointing me in the right direction and also to Bobby Gainher for all the help and advice he gave me as copy editor. But many others have also greatly assisted by providing pictures or checking my draft chapters and making many helpful corrections and suggestions. They are: Reg Barlow, Martin Barraclough, John Blake, Alan Bramson, Sandra Brind, Iain Browning, Steve Burr, Ray Deacon, Neville Duke, Veronica Dunne, David Emmerson, David Exton, John Fricker, Michael Graydon, Rod Hall-Jones, Rachel Huxford, Michael Jones, 'Min' Larkin, Bob Lightfoot, Ian Macfadyen, Chrissy and Gordon Morris, Rob Neil, Alan Pollock, 'Mo' Short, Michael Turner, John Urmston, Michiel Vogelpoel, Ken Wallis, Nigel Walpole and Andrew Wight-Boycott.

The book is sold for the benefit of the Royal Air Force Benevolent Fund.

For once you have tasted flight, you will for ever walk the earth with your eyes turned skywards, for there you have been, and there you will long to return.

Leonardo da Vinci 1452–1519

Chapter 1
In the Beginning

As a small boy I spent most of my time building, flying and crashing model aeroplanes. Most of my school holidays were spent in the company of a near neighbour, John Urmston, who shared the same passion. We were at kindergarten together and have been good friends ever since; he will feature significantly as my story unfolds. He designed a 5 ft span Tiger Moth, powered by a 7.5 cc petrol engine which we built together – it even had movable controls from the cockpit, but I have to admit that he built all the difficult bits. The caption in my photograph album reads 'it even flew after a fashion', but John added in his own hand 'it flew bloody well!'

Each year I used to follow the reports of the King's Cup Air Race, which at that time was a major national event well covered in the newspapers and I

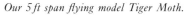
Our 5 ft span flying model Tiger Moth.

My mother and Jim Breakall after my first flight in 1935.

hoped, one day, that I might be able to take part in it. The only other ambition I had at that time was to own one of those magnificent Mercedes sports cars.

My father flew with the Royal Flying Corps (RFC) in the First World War and although he subsequently became a doctor, he retained his interest in flying and was on the committee of our local flying club at West Malling in Kent, which was very close to where we lived at Wateringbury. In my school holidays I used to cycle up to the small grass airfield, which at that time consisted of just two hangars, a club house and a squash court. I spent many happy hours watching the flying and wandering around the hangars. Then one day, when I was ten years old, the Chief Flying Instructor, Jim Breakall (another ex-RFC flyer), asked me if I would like to go up. We flew in one of the club's Gipsy Moths, G-AACZ, and from that moment in 1935 I knew exactly what I wanted to do with my life – I wanted to fly aeroplanes. I found out later that the flight had been arranged by my parents who had agreed to let Jim decide when the time was right.

I also had some rather grandiose ideas about my future – I thought I would become a famous aircraft designer and test pilot – but it was not until I went to Cambridge on a short wartime course that I realized I did not have the brains to become either.

In the summer term of 1938 I was recuperating at home after an operation. My younger brother Dick was at the same prep school, Fonthill near East Grinstead, and my father and I thought it would be fun to fly over the school and drop a message to Dick by parachute. I spent hours developing the parachute consisting of a message, some cigarette cards – we all collected them in those days – and some coins to act as ballast, all suspended from the canopy which was a handkerchief. I tested this device by throwing it out of a top-storey window at home. On the great day we flew in a Spartan three-seater, an open-cockpit biplane with the pilot in the front cockpit and two passengers in a separate open tandem cockpit behind. When we found the school we realized a cricket match was taking place, but the game was immediately suspended whilst the players and spectators watched us swoop down and drop the

A DH Gipsy Moth, similar to the one in which I enjoyed my first flight in 1935. Aeroplane magazine/ www.aeroplanemonthly.com

parachute. The arrangement we had with the pilot was that I would throw it out when he gave the signal – his judgement was spot on because we saw the parachute land close to the middle of the pitch. Thus we inaugurated the first and only direct air mail to Fonthill and my brother was the local hero for the day.

The Spartan Three Seater showing the tandem open cockpit behind the pilot. Rob Neil

Messerschmitt Bf 108 at Lympne in 1938.

My father took me and Dick to the 1938 International Air Rally at Lympne, where I saw for the first time an aircraft with a retractable undercarriage, the attractive Messerschmitt Bf 108 Taifun. Also in the line-up was Alex Henshaw's Mew Gull, G-AEXF, winner of the 1938 King's Cup Air Race. I followed Alex Henshaw's aviation exploits with great interest, particularly his

Alex Henshaw's Mew Gull at Lympne in 1938.

remarkable 1939 flight in the Mew Gull from England to Cape Town and back in 4½ days, setting a solo record which has never been beaten. He became a Spitfire test pilot during the War. The Mew Gull is still around, but sadly, Alex died in February 2007 at the age of 94.

During the summer holidays of 1940 my brother and I remember watching the Battle of Britain being fought overhead – we actually saw a Heinkel 111 being shot down. It was being circled by a number of fighters whilst it attempted to carry out a forced landing at West Malling which, by then, was one of the main RAF airfields in the Battle. The previous year I had gone to school at Marlborough where, initially, I joined the Officers Training Corps, but I did not enjoy pretending to be a soldier, although I did like rifle shooting and became a member of the college VIII. In 1941 the Air Training Corps was founded and the school formed one of the first squadrons, No. 529 (Marlborough Schools) Squadron which, of course, I joined, rising to the dizzy rank of corporal. We were given an old Puss Moth to play with and I just enjoyed tinkering with it and imagining I was flying it. On many afternoons I would cycle to one of the nearby airfields (Upavon, Netheravon or Membury) with my ATC uniform in the saddle bag, crawl through the hedge and pretend to be on one of the ATC camps. So much for the security of the day – on one occasion I actually talked my way into flying in an Oxford.

We had the occasional air raid warning at Marlborough and on those occasions we would go to the cellars and sleep in bunk beds. One night I was sleeping in a top bunk when I fell out of bed and bruised a rib. We did not know it at the time, but a bomb had landed about five miles away so I was able to claim that I was the school's first air raid casualty. We had our own Home Guard unit at Marlborough and I am proud to be able to say I really was a member of Dad's Army. On the whole I found school very frustrating because I felt I was just marking time before I could join the RAF.

Soon after the Battle of Britain our house was requisitioned to accommodate some Canadian soldiers, so we rented a house at Maidstone. I soon found that during school holidays, as an ATC

My First World War uniform of the Marlborough College Officers Training Corps.

cadet, I could usually scrounge some Link Trainer flying at RAF Detling which was within cycle range of our new home. The Link Trainer was the forerunner of the modern simulator and was an excellent device for learning to fly on instruments. This proved to have been a great advantage to me once I started flying.

From Marlborough we went to an ATC camp at RAF Lyneham which I thoroughly enjoyed. I was so impressed with the Station Warrant Officer that I decided that there was no point in becoming an officer as it was obvious to me that the RAF was run by the NCOs. However, that notion did not last long because shortly afterwards I applied for a place at Cambridge on a 'University Short Course for Potential Officers'. My second choice was for St Andrew's, but I was fortunate in being selected for Cambridge where I was accommodated in my father's rooms at Christ's College. I don't know how he fixed this, but it must have been more than a mere coincidence.

I read mechanical sciences and the course, beginning in October 1943, lasted for six months. During that time we did first-year work and, if we decided to return after the War, we would be able to start with second-year work. It was a valuable six months and a very good deal. We were members of the Cambridge University Air Squadron and occasionally flew in their Tiger Moths at Marshall's Airfield. I shared rooms with a colleague who did not have the same educational advantages I had been given, but it was obvious that he was intellectually my superior, so much so that I gave up all thoughts of ever becoming an aircraft designer. In any case, by then I wanted to be a pilot so much that I had no 'Plan B' – if for any reason I had not succeeded at any stage of my training, I had absolutely no idea what I would have done. As I neared the end of my time at Cambridge I could hardly wait to join the RAF.

Chapter 2
Joining Up

In April 1944 I joined the RAF and was immediately posted to No. 6 Aircrew Reception Centre at Scarborough. We were billeted in the Prince of Wales Hotel at the top of the cliff. My room was a small attic bedroom with a very low window sill which had probably been a staff bedroom, but to me it was bliss because I could lie in bed and watch the sea. The east coast was a restricted area at the time so there were no visitors to the town. The next door hotel was occupied by an evacuated teachers' training college – which perhaps accounted for the rumour that our tea was laced with bromide. Although we experienced the expected military discipline and a certain amount of 'bull', I found the training less irksome than the discipline at boarding school – perhaps because, at last, I had reached the first rung of the ladder leading to becoming a pilot.

From Scarborough I went to No. 4 Elementary Flying Training School (EFTS) at Brough near Hull for 'grading', in which we were given ten hours or so of Tiger Moth flying to see if we were suitable to undertake flying training. I went solo after seven and a half hours which was about average, although I did have a problem with landing. I remember doing guard duty one night and spending most of the time going over and over in my mind the landing process. To my amazement I had no trouble the next day and it was then that I was sent solo. I subsequently used this technique several times in the future when I had problems – like sorting out slow rolls. I vividly remember that first solo as the most thrilling event of my life to date and I can picture now the empty cockpit in front of me as I climbed away from the airfield. For some unaccountable reason I found myself singing the theme of a Chopin nocturne – the one in E flat major – at the top of my voice. Whenever I hear the nocturne now I think of that momentous event. Although I passed the grading process, my only regret is that we were not issued with log books at Grading School and I never thought of recording each flight – so it all has to remain a memory. One of the instructors, an experienced pilot, told me that he still always got a kick every time he started a take-off – that same kick never left me throughout my flying life.

One day a B-17 Flying Fortress arrived, presumably for work to be carried out on it at the Blackburn factory at Brough. All the cadets gathered round to see it taxi in. As the engines were shut down we walked towards it and I was amazed to look through the bomb aimer's window in the nose to see a pair of shapely female legs at the pilot's seat. A young Air Transport Auxiliary pilot got out and as far as we could tell she was flying the aircraft alone. We were mightily impressed.

Unfortunately for us there were more pilots in the training pipeline than the RAF needed at that stage of the War, so we were offered a choice of four trades to kill time whilst we waited for the next stage of training at an EFTS. I chose motorcyclist because I thought it was the only one of the four where I wouldn't have an NCO on my back all day. I therefore found myself on a course at No. 8 School of Technical Training at Weeton, near Blackpool, where I spent an enjoyable month learning how to be a dispatch rider. At the end of the course I could ride a motorcycle and fly an aeroplane, aged eighteen, but could not yet drive a car — just like my father who could fly before he could drive.

I was posted to the HQ of No. 75 Signals Wing based, or so I was told, at Keston, Bromley. I arrived one afternoon with my kitbag over my shoulder only to find a large bomb crater and no Headquarters. A passing pedestrian told me the HQ had been destroyed by a V2 rocket the previous month and had been relocated at Broadstairs, so I made my way to Victoria Station where the Railway Transport Officer gave me a warrant and off I went to the seaside.

The Wing HQ was based in Stone House Preparatory School which, I presumed, had been evacuated elsewhere. I was billeted in the gym together with twenty or so other airmen and my job was to take urgently needed spares to the coastal radar stations between Walton on the Naze and the Isle of Wight. My sturdy steed was a 500 cc BSA side-valve motorcycle. We had a few Harley Davidsons in the MT section, but unfortunately we sprogs were not allowed anywhere near them. It amuses me these days to go to an agricultural show and to find my machine amongst the vintage exhibits. We were not issued with any proper clothing so my father, by now a captain in the Royal

My father proudly wearing his First World War medals and Royal Flying Corps observer's wing on his Second World War Royal Army Medical Corps uniform.

Army Medical Corps proudly wearing his RFC observer wing, made me some excellent waterproof kit out of an army gas cape which must have fallen off the back of a lorry.

There were no signposts in those days and I always found it difficult to navigate my way through London on the way to the east coast. If I got lost my technique was to go downhill to try and find the Thames, identify a bridge and then start again. One very cold wet November morning about 2.00 am I was hopelessly lost, but fortunately I found a friendly policeman. 'Excuse me, officer,' I said, 'could you please tell me the way to the river?' I must have been looking very cold and miserable – which I was – because he put his hand on my shoulder and said, 'I wouldn't do that if I were you, lad.'

Those were the days of the dreaded V1 Doodlebugs. I remember listening to the distinctive sounds of their engines, and then the apprehensive silence when the engine cut and one waited for the inevitable explosion, hoping it wasn't going to be too close. After an enjoyable three months rushing around on my motorbike I was, at last, about to begin my flying training.

Chapter 3
Flying at Last

I arrived at No. 11 EFTS at Scone, near Perth, in February 1945. This was my first visit to Scotland and I very soon realized what friendly generous people the Scots were, quite different from the music hall caricatures. We were billeted in a hotel by the River Tay called The Durn; it was a delightful spot. This, together with some eighty hours of wonderful flying, added up to a memorable time for me. I count myself very lucky to have been one of the last of the generation of pilots who were taught to fly with our heads in the fresh air, with no radio, no navigation aids except a map and wobbly compass, and no Air Traffic Control – and all this over such beautiful countryside. I soon found that I particularly enjoyed aerobatics and, not surprisingly, I was determined to become a fighter pilot.

I had originally hoped to do my flying training in Canada or Rhodesia under the Empire Air Training Scheme, or even in the United States, but so many of my contemporaries who were training in those countries at that time had their courses cancelled. It was our good fortune that we were able to continue whilst so many fell by the wayside.

In May 1945 we were posted to No. 1 Course of 19 FTS at Cranwell to fly the Harvard. In fact we were the first flying course to 'march in' to the College towards the end of the War. We do not call ourselves 'Cranwellians' because our course was to last only six months and this bore little comparison to the pre-war two year Cranwell course. When VJ Day was declared on 15th August – my twentieth birthday – in 1945 we obviously celebrated the occasion, but I have to admit to a slight sense of disappointment when I realized I would not be able to fly operationally in the War, but then perhaps that is why I am still alive today. We were commissioned and received our wings on 19th October 1945 from Air Marshal Sir John Slessor, whose son John was a fellow cadet and received his wings from his father at the same time.

My hopes of becoming a fighter pilot were dashed when I was posted to the Transport Command holding unit and sent on indefinite leave. At this stage in

The 19 FTS Graduation Parade in October 1945, the first flying course to graduate at Cranwell since the War.

one's career the thought of a long leave was the last thing one wanted and it was made worse by the thought of eventually having to fly transport aircraft, probably Dakotas, the exact opposite of what I had hoped for.

But salvation was at hand. Five months after leaving Cranwell, Christopher Blount, a fellow cadet on No. 1 Course, was already at the Mosquito Night Fighter Operational Training Unit at RAF East Moor, a few miles north of York. He invited me to stay for a weekend and so I drove up from Kent in my car, a BSA three wheeler, to join him. I was so impressed with what he told me about the Mosquito that I decided I would approach the Chief Flying Instructor (CFI) on the Monday morning and ask him if he would apply for me to join his course. I was astonished when the CFI, a Wing Commander, said, 'Can you start tomorrow?' I replied, 'No sir, because I will have to fetch my uniform which is at home in Kent, but I can start on Wednesday.' And so I did.

At the end of the three week ground school phase the authority for me to start flying had still not come through, so the CFI flew me in his own Mosquito to the Holding Unit at Snaith to try to persuade the staff to re-post me from Transport Command to Fighter Command. He was not immediately successful, nevertheless he took it upon himself to allow me to start the flying phase, even though I was technically still on leave from Transport Command. I will always remain extremely grateful to that Wing Commander, Bill Gill, for giving a young Pilot Officer the chance to fulfil his ambitions because, if I had bent one of his aircraft, I'm sure he would have been in serious trouble. I met

Air Marshal Sir John Slessor presents my wings.

him many years later when I was an Air Commodore and he was a retired Air
Vice-Marshal and took the opportunity then to thank him for what he had done
for me. He simply said, 'My thanks are to see you where you are now.'

I believe we were the first students to train on Mosquitoes having had no
prior training on twin-engined aircraft. The Mosquito was delightful to fly,
but it did have a tendency to swing badly on take-off or landing – the answer

was not to let it. I well remember my first solo on the type because when my instructor, Squadron Leader Basil Primavesi, got out of the aircraft and sent me off, I discovered I had forgotten to bring a map with me so, although I flew for an hour, I took great care not to lose sight of the airfield. Needless to say I never admitted this stupid error to my instructor.

After three weeks leave I was posted to No. 264 Night Fighter Squadron equipped with Mosquito Mk 36s at Church Fenton, still in Yorkshire, where, lo and behold, two days later my posting came through – to Bomber Command. Needless to say things were soon sorted out and together with my navigator, 'Red' Hall, we set off for eighteen very happy months flying together on our first squadron. We were the first post-war qualified crews to reach squadrons and I was very conscious of the fact that everyone else on the squadron had a row of gallantry and campaign medals together with a wealth of wartime experience. I realized I had a long way to go before I was going to be able to catch up with them.

Shortly after my arrival on the squadron we were detached to Lübeck on the Baltic coast for an armament practice camp. I remember flying over Hamburg and being moved by the appalling devastation caused by Allied bombing. It was two days before my twenty-first birthday and my squadron commander allowed me to take a Mosquito home to West Malling for the weekend to celebrate the occasion. Two months later the squadron moved to yet another station in Yorkshire – Linton-on-Ouse.

My first photograph of Mosquito Mk 36s of No. 264 Night Fighter Squadron.

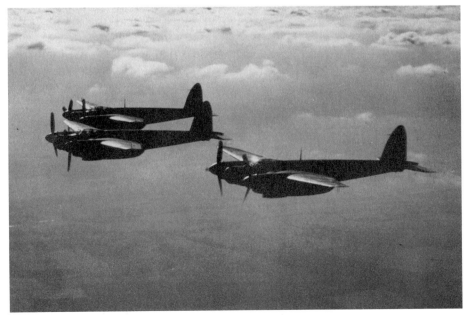

My navigator 'Red' Hall, left, on No. 264 Squadron.

My parents had given me my first car, the 1933 BSA Three Wheeler, for an advanced 21st birthday present. This was very second hand and cost £110. It was in good condition except for the tyres which were almost down to the canvas. The War was still on and tyres were very difficult to obtain, especially 19 inch tyres. The only way I managed to get hold of any was by visiting scrap yards and hoping to find some with more tread than I had on my own at the time. Punctures and even tyre bursts were frequent occurrences. I named the car 'IKANOPIT II' and proudly painted the name on the bonnet. It was powered by a 1,000 cc V twin cylinder air cooled engine which tended to seize up if the car was driven faster than 35 mph, although it would usually quickly free itself after cooling off at the roadside.

One day I had a minor fire when an oily rag which I had carelessly left between the cylinders ignited; the problem was quickly solved by removing the rag. However, the incident convinced me that it would be a good idea always to carry a fire extinguisher, so I promptly obtained one. The very next time I used the car I was returning from a pub crawl when it seriously caught fire. The carburettor was positioned between the two cylinders and the fuel pipe connecting it to the tank broke. Consequently petrol poured out on to the hot cylinders and the inevitable happened. Luckily the car was fitted with a fuel cock so I was able to turn off the flow of petrol before using the new extinguisher which quickly put out the inferno. I have carried a fire extinguisher in my cars ever since, not just to be able to put my own fires out, but perhaps to be able to help someone else in trouble. The fact that this serious fire happened on the first run with the new extinguisher made me think that this might be more than a mere coincidence. Subsequently, over the years, several other incidents have occurred which led me to believe that perhaps someone was looking after me; they used to call them guardian angels. Why should they bother? Perhaps there is a purpose in 'fate' being so kind. If so, I haven't yet found out what it is.

Cars in those days were very simple and easy to maintain. I had several breakdowns and usually managed to solve the problems myself; I was even able to remove the engine and de-coke it, something the amateur couldn't even contemplate with today's sophisticated electronic wizardry, hydraulic systems, fuel injection etc.

All this was well illustrated when I was about to drive through London on the way to our home in Kent (no M25 in those days) when there was an enormous bang and the most horrid noise coming from the engine. On lifting the bonnet it was obvious what had happened – the exhaust valve of one of the cylinders had disappeared, presumably it had fallen into the cylinder and had been pounded by the piston. In fact the cotter pin holding the valve in place had failed. Nothing daunted, I took the cylinder head off by the roadside, removed the exhaust valve which had been pounded into an 's' shaped lump of metal, and put the head back. I then removed the sparking plug to reduce the resistance caused by compression. When I started the engine the air rushing in and out of the sparking plug hole created a loud and most peculiar noise; consequently I received some very funny looks whenever we stopped at traffic lights etc. It never occurred to me to seek assistance from a garage and I drove like this through London and reached home without further trouble on one cylinder. I have kept that valve ever since as a momento of an exciting journey.

The Mosquito was an astonishing venture. The Air Ministry policy at the beginning of the War was for bombers to be made of metal and to be heavily armed, which naturally resulted in slow aircraft. Geoffrey De Havilland thought that a wooden unarmed aircraft, which would be light and fast, could be built by the many highly skilled cabinet makers currently being mis-employed on munitions. Furthermore, suitable wood was available. The first prototype flew in November 1940, less than eleven months after design work began, and Mosquitoes became operational the following year, a process that nowadays takes at least ten times as long. They were faster than the current German fighters and they had the range to take a meaningful bomb load to Berlin. Nearly 8,000 Mosquitoes were built in forty-three versions and they served in every command and theatre, staying in service until 1961 – a true success story.

Already at Linton were two other squadrons, Nos 64 and 65, equipped with single-seat Hornet day fighters. These were splendid aircraft which, to me, were rather like sports car versions of their older big brother, the Mosquito. They were said to be the fastest piston-engined aircraft in service anywhere in the world. They had 'handed' propellers going round in opposite directions to each other so that there was no tendency to swing on take-off. There were serviceability problems with this new aircraft and the hours the squadron pilots were allowed to fly each month were severely restricted. Consequently outsiders were not allowed to fly them.

I was still making model aircraft at that time and decided to make for myself a 1/72 scale model of a Hornet. I was keen to make the cockpit details as accurately as possible so I went across to 64 Squadron's hangar, climbed in to one of their aircraft and started sketching the cockpit. I should, of course, have asked permission; furthermore I failed to notice a Squadron Leader's flag painted on the side of the fuselage. No wonder, therefore, that a few moments later a very angry squadron commander arrived and shouted up to me in the cockpit, 'What the hell are you doing in my aircraft?' When I explained what I was up to his whole attitude turned through 180 degrees and he said, 'It's a funny thing. I've been trying to persuade De Havillands to give me a model Hornet, but to no avail.' I cheekily replied, 'Well sir, if you let me fly one of your aircraft you can have my model.' We both kept to the deal and shortly afterwards I flew a Hornet three years to the day after joining the RAF. I believe I was the only outsider on the station who managed to fly one of those wonderful aircraft during that period. It was my first experience in a single-seat aircraft and was very memorable.

A DH Hornet Mk 1 – The ultimate piston-engined fighter? Aeroplane Magazine/www.aeroplanemonthly.com

The Hornet was a joy to fly; its performance on one engine was far superior to that of the non-aerobatic Mosquito and I therefore amused myself by doing some rolls on one engine before I landed back. No wonder I have heard it referred to as a 'Hot-Rod Mini-Mossie'. Sadly, no example of this magnificent aircraft exists today. Someone, somewhere, must have destroyed the last Hornet without realising what he was doing.

At that time, 1946, I became very interested in helicopters and joined the Helicopter Association of Great Britain. I had seen my mother flying in an autogiro at an Alan Cobham air display before the War and there was something about rotary wing flying that had always intrigued me. I stayed with a friend who lived near Eastleigh, Southampton, where the RAF was experimenting with the American Sikorsky R4, and persuaded their senior pilot, Alan Marsh, to give me some instruction in one of these fascinating machines – I have enjoyed helicopter flying ever since. I just felt that there was a tremendous future for helicopters because of their ability to get in and out of very small sites, almost regardless of the surface conditions. Sadly, Alan was killed in the experimental tri-rotor Air Horse a few years later. One of the reasons that I have enjoyed flying helicopters is that I regarded them as a challenge. The handling techniques are very different from those of fixed-wing aircraft and with the early machines you had to work at them all the time – you could not trim them 'hands-off' and just relax. Also during this period I obtained a Private Pilot's Licence flying an Auster.

I considered applying to transfer to helicopters, but at that time they were very much in their infancy and the career prospects within the RAF were slim. I also toyed with the idea of becoming an airline pilot, but that thought didn't last very long because I was enjoying flying the Mosquito too much.

Sikorsky R4 Helicopter – the Hoverfly. Military Aircraft Photographs

On reflection I think I would have been very bored just flying straight and level, hour after hour, with the autopilot doing all the work. Also I was already developing a taste for flying different types of aircraft and, as the years rolled by, I was able to follow up that interest.

Before I left 264 Squadron in January 1948 the squadron was to move twice more, first to Wittering and then to Coltishall. Four stations in eighteen months. We thought little of it at the time, but if that had happened in this day and age the Ministry of Defence would no doubt have be sued by some airman for infringement of his human rights, or whatever.

Chapter 4
Payback Time

Having enjoyed my flying training towards the end of the War so much, and my first tour on a Mosquito night fighter squadron just after the War ended, I decided that I would like to put something back into flying. Thinking this could best be done by becoming a test pilot or by instructing, I soon realised I did not have the academic skills to become a test pilot, so I applied for the course at the Central Flying School (CFS) at RAF Little Rissington to become a Qualified Flying Instructor (QFI). I admit there was a certain attraction in going to CFS at that time because the course included flying the Lancaster,

Tiger Moths of CFS in the low-flying area near Stow-on-the-Wold. Christopher Blount

Mosquito, Spitfire and Vampire in addition to the Harvard and Tiger Moth on which one would learn the techniques of instruction. It would be a fantastic opportunity for an inexperienced pilot like me to fly three new representative front line types.

It is important for flying instructors to have an understanding of the handling requirements of those aircraft which their students are likely to be flying. These four operational types were typical of the current heavy bombers (Lancaster), multi-role aircraft (Mosquito), piston-engine fighters (Spitfire) and jet fighters (Vampire). Most of the students on the CFS course would be experienced in at least one of the roles, but few would have had the chance to fly all of them.

I began the six month course in January 1948 and again I was very conscious of my inexperience compared to the majority of the other students who had wartime operational flying in their log books. I believe one of the best ways to improve a skill is to try to teach it, and certainly on this course one really did learn about the finer points of flying. I had had few opportunities to do any aerobatics since my flying training days, so I particularly enjoyed polishing up the various manoeuvres and was very thrilled to be awarded the Clarkson Trophy at the end of the course for the best aerobatic pilot.

Aerobatics are very important skills for any pilot to acquire. It is not just a matter of being able to give an exciting display; rather they teach pilots co-ordination skills and, most importantly, they are a method by which pilots can learn how to recover an aircraft safely after finding themselves in an unusual attitude. This may be caused, for example, by some form of mechanical failure, losing control in a thunderstorm or by simply mishandling the aircraft. By being competent at aerobatics pilots know how to identify the problem quickly and then recover rapidly and safely from any attitude, even at night or in cloud when flying on instruments. I consider that such training is essential, even for those civilian pilots who are training to be airline pilots, because it is unlikely that they will go through their entire careers without finding themselves in an unusual and potentially dangerous attitude at least once. Aerobatics also help students to fly very accurately which is an essential requirement for a good pilot – and they also happen to be great fun, although some would question that statement.

I had, of course, already flown the Mosquito, but the other three were a very exciting prospect. The first time I flew a jet aircraft was when I flew the single-seat Vampire Mk 3. It was a beautiful evening and I clearly remember the wonderful view from the cockpit, the complete lack of vibration coupled with a very low noise level and of wheeling this delightful little aircraft around the clouds over the Cotswold Hills. I am reminded of John Magee's remarkable poem which describes the sheer joy of flying far better than I possibly could. I certainly 'danced the skies with laughter-silvered wings' on that occasion. Sadly, he was killed in a Spitfire mid-air collision in 1941. He was just nineteen.

High Flight

Oh! I have slipped the surly bonds of Earth
And danced the skies on laughter-silvered wings;
Sunward I've climbed, and joined the tumbling mirth
Of sun-split clouds – and done a hundred things
You have not dreamed of – wheeled and soared and swung
High in the sunlit silence. Hov'ring there,
I've chased the shouting wind along, and flung
My eager craft through footless halls of air
Up, up the long, delirious burning blue
I've topped the wind-swept heights with easy grace,
Where never lark, or even eagle flew –
And, while with silent, lifting mind I've trod
The high un-trespassed sanctity of space,
Put out my hand and touched the face of God.

Pilot Officer John Magee

It was very exciting for me to be able to fly the Spitfire which must be one of the most charismatic fighters ever built. It caused much amusement in the crew room to watch fellow students take off on their first flights because they invariably wobbled a bit just after take-off as the undercarriage was raised. The reason was because the lever to raise the wheels was on the right hand side of the cockpit, so one had to change hands by taking the right hand off the stick to raise the wheels whilst replacing it with the left hand which had been holding the throttle lever. As the elevators were very sensitive, the tyro's wobble was almost inevitable.

There is another reason why I remember that first Spitfire flight and it is one that I am not at all proud of. One of the problems of landing a single-engine fighter is that there is a great big engine in front which blocks the view of the runway when landing – which is why most pilots fly a curved approach so that they can see the runway until the last few hundred feet. A fundamental rule of flying is that one must always keep a good lookout for other aircraft, but I failed to do so on this occasion. I was concentrating so much on making an accurate curved approach that I forgot to check that no one else was flying a straight-in approach at the same time. The first thing I knew was when I flew under a Harvard that was so close I could hear its engine. Apparently the runway controller in his caravan at the end of the runway could have fired a red Very light to tell me to go round again, but did not do so in case both aircraft took the same action and collided. I never ever made that mistake again.

My first solo in a Lancaster was memorable for a totally different reason. My instructor, Graham Hulse, wanted to send me solo, but the flight engineer had been flying all morning and was due for a break and a bite to eat, so Graham said, 'I will be your flight engineer, but to prove that I can have no influence on your flying I will lie down behind you so that I can still see the engine gauges.' And he did! Graham made a name for himself when he subsequently baled out of a Meteor when it broke up around him during a Battle of Britain air display at Little Rissington in 1950. Sadly he was killed in Korea, but not until he had shot down two Mig 15s.

From CFS I was posted to the RAF College at Cranwell in July 1948 and, together with Christopher Blount who was also on the same CFS course, I arrived one Sunday evening to book in to the Officers' Mess. Needless to say the first thing we did was to go into the bar which was then fairly crowded. No sooner had we entered the room than an impressive-looking fellow immediately came up to us and said, 'My name's Atcherley, what's yours?' This turned out to be Air Commodore 'Batchy' Atcherley, the Commandant of the College. I was very impressed with this gesture and vowed to try and follow his example in the future when new arrivals appeared for the first time.

We were to instruct on the basic phase flying the new Percival Prentice, a descendant of the Mew Gull that had intrigued me so much as a youngster. The Prentice, however, had little similarity to that splendid racer. The Air Ministry had decided that, for the first time, basic trainers should have side by side seating so that the instructor could see exactly what his student was doing. It was also decided to put a third seat behind the pilots so that another student could gain experience by watching and listening to what was going on in the front. The engine was to be the relatively low-powered Gipsy Queen. I visited the factory at Luton and was surprised to learn that, when tested for strength, the wing did not break until a simulated load of 13.4g was applied – i.e. 13.4 times the weight of the aircraft – which meant that the wing was stronger than its designed intended strength. All these factors added up to a rather heavy under-powered aircraft with an uninspiring performance. I also think it was one of the ugliest aircraft ever built by a British manufacturer. Nevertheless I enjoyed instructing on the Prentice and personally liked the side by side concept. The third seat was never used as intended, but it was quite useful for ferrying people about. I found instructing every bit as rewarding as I had hoped it would be – seeing a student go off on his first solo, whilst hoping he would come back safely, was a very satisfying experience.

There were many opportunities for instructors to develop their skills by flying with other instructors or by flying solo; this was known as Staff Continuation Training or SCT. On one SCT sortie I thought I would see how many turns of a spin I could carry out before recovering at the minimum permitted altitude of 3,000 ft. Flying alone to minimize the weight, I managed to struggle up to 12,000 ft a few miles south of Cranwell, which I could clearly see. There was a strong wind blowing and I travelled some distance during the thirty turns of the spin that I managed and I remember actually reading my map as I spun downwards. I have often wondered how many pilots have been able to read their maps during a spin.

Knowing the Prentice was very strong I also used to bunt the aircraft from level flight, pushing forward on the stick to do the first half of a loop, but going downwards and finishing up upside down. A bunt is an aviator's term for an 'outside loop' where the pilot is on the outside of the manoeuvre and experiencing negative instead of positive g loading. Interesting, but not very comfortable. In the Prentice I could not complete the second half of the bunt going upwards because the engine would not keep running when inverted. For a spot of variety I would sometimes stop the engine and glide down in blissful silence. I took a photograph of a fellow instructor, Peter Breton, flying a Prentice in this way, with the propeller stopped, and accompanied in formation by another Prentice. In order to keep in formation with Peter the second pilot needed to retain power which, of course, would make him go faster, so to slow down he lowered flap, thereby creating more drag. This resulted in the aircraft flying slightly nose down – an interesting demonstration of aerodynamics.

I have always felt that the few hours flying those different operational aircraft at CFS did my flying more good than hundreds of hours on a single type. My theory was well illustrated when John Fricker visited Cranwell in 1949 to write an article about the Prentice for the magazine *Aeroplane*. At the time he only had about thirty-five hours in his log book, but he flew the Prentice far better than any student of similar experience that I had flown with. Many years later I discussed this with him and we put it down to the fact that he had already handled a wide variety of aircraft, even if only for a short time on each one.

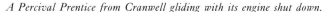

A Percival Prentice from Cranwell gliding with its engine shut down.

Batchy Atcherley was somewhat of a hero figure. He had been one of the Schneider Trophy pilots in 1929 when he broke the world air speed record in a Supermarine S6 seaplane at 370 mph. He was also well known for various aeronautical antics and was a member of the CFS formation aerobatic team in the pre-war Hendon flying displays. At Cranwell he had somehow managed to acquire a Messerschmitt Bf 108 Taifun, the sporting aircraft which I had first seen at Lympne ten years earlier. He would invariably be the first airborne in the mornings and frequently beat us up in his Taifun during morning parades.

One afternoon Batchy Atcherley wanted to fly down to Hendon in a Prentice and asked for a volunteer to bring the aircraft back. Chris Blount and I were both free that afternoon so we volunteered. I sat in the back and Chris alongside the Commandant who, shortly after take-off, opened his briefcase, took out *The Times* and proceeded to read it, periodically looking over the side and saying something like, 'Old so-and-so lives there – we had a splendid day's shooting with him last year.' Not once did he look at a map, he just seemed to be navigating from one country house to the next. When we got to Hendon there was a very strong crosswind from the right which was a bit of a problem for the Prentice which had a large fin and rudder; consequently, on the ground, it tended to turn into wind like a weathercock once it slowed down. It was in fact very difficult to turn the aircraft downwind when at taxying speed if the crosswind was strong. In this instance we were approaching the end of the runway after landing and Batchy wanted to turn left, but nothing happened and the aircraft continued to go straight on. Chris and I were sure we were going to finish up in the hedge, but Batchy quickly assessed the situation, switched off the ignition switches and put on full right rudder and right brake, causing the aircraft to ground loop to the right. After 270 degrees he was facing the way he originally wanted to go so he switched the switches back on just before the engine stopped and carried on as if nothing had happened. All this only took a few seconds and we concluded that if a pilot could think that quickly he deserved to live another day.

We used to have an annual 'College Run' in which the cadets, and all the staff under forty years of age, had to take part. It was a cross-country run and as far as I can remember it was only about 3 miles. Rather stupidly I tried hard and came through the finishing gate near the front when I was promptly collared by the Assistant Commandant, Group Captain 'Doggie' Oliver, who said, 'You are now officer in charge of cross-country running.' I was never a particularly keen sportsman, although I did enjoy riding, swimming and the occasional game of squash, but I disliked running intensely. Of all the sports, I had to be given this one to look after. Many years later, when I was a group captain, I attended a graduation ceremony at Cranwell as a guest. After the parade I was wandering around the College corridors looking at the various group photographs and I came across my cross-country team of 1949. I was in uniform and one of the cadets saw me and asked, 'What was it like flying in the olden days sir?' It was a delightful question which I answered as best as I could, although I didn't really feel that I was qualified to reply.

I was however, a very keen rifle and pistol shot and was much happier when I found myself officer in charge of those activities. I used to spend up to six weeks at Bisley each year, quite successfully – I even got into the RAF pistol VIII squad, but failed to make the team on the day. I soon realized that all this time away from my primary job must be interfering with my flying career, so I gave up rifle shooting and just concentrated on the pistol which was not nearly as time-consuming as the rifle.

During the leave periods there were all sorts of activities for the cadets to take part in. On one occasion I and three other officers took a group of cadets to the Parachute Training School at Upper Heyford for a short parachute course. I was intrigued to find out how soldiers who had never flown were taught to jump out of a perfectly serviceable aircraft. I also wanted to see how frightened I was going to be – as a sort of masochism, you might say. The ground training was quite alarming, especially when one had to jump from the roof of a hanger, the descent being controlled by a 'fan' – if one could cope with that the flying part should be easy to handle. Our first of two jumps from a balloon was also unnerving because, with no slipstream to open the parachute quickly, you fell a couple of hundred feet or so before the parachute fully deployed – the rest is bliss. We followed that with two jumps from a Dakota which were very exciting.

On another occasion we took a group of cadets to Scharfoldendorf in the Black Mountains for some gliding. This was an ex-Luftwaffe gliding school equipped with the original German gliders, the airfield being on top of a ridge where one could enjoy some excellent ridge soaring. After the First World War Germany was forbidden by the Treaty of Versailles to have an air force, but they got round the problem in part by forming a number of gliding schools and developing some very fine gliders, thus enabling pilots to learn how to fly. However, in 1935 Germany illegally repudiated the disarmament clauses of the Treaty and announced that it had established a new air force, the Luftwaffe. A massive rearmament programme quickly followed and the rest is history. These gliding schools were retained during the Second World War and the RAF inherited some of them when the War was over.

I found gliding to be a very satisfying activity. I remember being briefed to fly for thirty minutes in a Grunau and I actually landed back after twenty-nine; this gave me a great sense of being in control of the elements. I loved gliding, but never took it up seriously because it tended to be a very time-consuming activity.

After two very happy years at Cranwell I was posted back to CFS at Little Rissington as a staff instructor. I had two weeks leave before taking up my new appointment and one evening I took my parents out for a drink at the Royal Oak at Wrotham. Whilst I was buying them a drink at the bar, someone came up to me and said, 'I couldn't help overhearing you talking about going from Cranwell to Little Rissington, because I'm also on leave, but am going from Little Rissington to Cranwell.' Somehow the conversation got round to horses and he said he would give me an introduction to a retired naval officer who lived near Little Rissington and who had some horses which he felt sure I would be able to help exercise.

Not long after arriving at Little Rissington I contacted the retired naval officer and was invited to stay for a weekend. No one had told me that he had a daughter, Katharine. A year to the day later we were married.

My first student at CFS was an army officer, Captain Claude Surgeon, who was going to be instructing on Austers at Middle Wallop and, because the RAF did not operate Austers, he brought his own aeroplane on the course. I think he was given to me as my student because I already had a civil licence on Austers so had some – but not very much – experience on the type. We had a hilarious six months together with me teaching him the techniques of instruction whilst he showed me how the Army flew their aircraft. Many years later I was house-hunting. When Katharine and I arrived at the front door of the house we were to view, I introduced myself by name, whereupon the owner said, 'You're not the Johnny Severne who taught me to be a QFI forty-eight years ago, are you?' It was indeed Claude and we bought the house.

I was also instructing students to become QFIs on the Harvard. At the same time I was able to indulge my passion for aerobatics. I did several 'instructor and pupil' acts at flying displays where one pilot does an exemplary manoeuvre whilst the other attempts to copy it and pretends to make a hash of it. I was the hasher.

Towards the end of the year CFS took possession of a Balliol Mk 1 for some trials and I was selected as the project officer to fly the aircraft, and this proved to be a most interesting experience. The Balliol was intended to replace the Harvard for advanced instruction and the Mk 1 was fitted with an Armstrong Siddeley Mamba turbo-prop engine. There were some development problems with the Mk 1 so the Mk 2 was produced with a Rolls Royce Merlin engine. In the event, the Mk 2 was ready for production first and that was the one that finally went into RAF service.

A Mamba had been fitted into the nose of a Dakota for in-flight trials and I experienced some engine handling instruction on this unique aircraft before being given a ten minute familiarization flight in the Mamba-powered Balliol Mk I by one of the test pilots. Gas turbines have a high idling speed and it is therefore necessary to have a variable pitch propeller, preferably one that can change pitch very quickly. If I remember correctly, this propeller changed pitch at 60° a second and consequently, if you flew along slowly with the engine throttled back and then slammed – literally – the throttle open, fuel would

The Prototype Mk 1 Balliol, the first single-engined turboprop in the world. Military Aircraft Photographs

immediately be pumped into the engine and the rapid pitch change would take up the power resulting in a dramatic acceleration. I remember flying on one occasion when a Harvard drew up alongside for a little formation flying. I thought I would show this chap what the Balliol could do so I slammed the throttle open and the aircraft shot forward to the amazement of the Harvard pilot. Many years later I read that this Balliol, VL892, was the world's first single-engine turbo-prop aircraft.

The Mamba-powered Balliol had one disconcerting habit. If the propeller detected an engine failure it would automatically feather, thus offering the least possible wind resistance whilst the pilot attempted a forced landing. Three months later I was delivering this aircraft to RAF Strubby. As I approached the airfield I was informed that no one else was in the circuit so I accelerated to high speed and did a very tight turn over the top when the engine decided to quit. I was immediately confronted with a stationary propeller in front of me, but I was over the airfield and it was just a question of selecting the most convenient runway to land on which was not, as it happened, the runway in use. As I came to a halt a car drew up and the Wing Commander Flying got out and said, 'Do you usually land those things like that?' What I had not realized was that, in concentrating on doing a safe landing, I had forgotten to turn off the fuel. Consequently kerosene had entered the hot engine and had produced a most impressive trail of white smoke. I suppose if I had watched a single-engine aircraft land on the wrong runway, with a stationary propeller and trailing white smoke, I too would have been a bit surprised.

Another aircraft we evaluated was the fully aerobatic Auster Aiglet in which Auster's chief test pilot, Ranald Porteous, used to do magnificent displays at the Farnborough Air Shows. I had the privilege of flying with him when he brought the Aiglet to CFS. The weather was not good, yet he went through his entire display routine under a 900 ft cloud base. Very impressive – and rather exciting.

On 21st September 1951 I witnessed a memorable event when Air Chief Marshal Sir James Robb, on his last flight as a serving officer, flew his personal Spitfire Mk XVI, SL 721, to CFS and handed it over to the Commandant, Air Commodore Selway. Sir James had learnt to fly at CFS, had become Chief Flying Instructor and also Commandant; at the time he was the Commander-in-Chief of the Western Union Air Forces. He had painted five stars on the side of the cockpit, one more than he was entitled to, but the same as his American counterpart. This was a remarkable aircraft having been lightened by taking out the guns and much of its armour plating. I subsequently flew it on a number of occasions and was surprised that it could climb to 40,000 ft quicker than a Vampire. This wonderful aircraft was subsequently sold by the Air Ministry for £150 and I next saw it outside a garage on the Sussex coast as a static exhibit. I still cannot understand why CFS let this unique aircraft be sold when I believe that, if the members of the Central Flying School Association had known it was to be sold, we could have easily raised the money

Air Chief Marshal Sir James Robb hands over his Spitfire Mk XVI to the Commandant of CFS after completing his last flight as a serving officer.

for it to be the permanent property of CFS. It has subsequently been bought by an American who has restored it to flying condition and is probably now worth several hundred thousand pounds.

By this time CFS no longer had a variety of operational aircraft for the students to fly, but we did have a flight of two-seat Gloster Meteor Mk 7s so that the students could experience jet flying up to solo standard if they had not already done so. I was keen to get on to the Meteor flight, not just because I wanted to instruct on jets, but because I thought that would enhance my chances of being posted back to an operational jet fighter squadron after my time at CFS. In fact I was able to join the Meteor flight some eight months after arriving back at Little Rissington and this proved to be one of the most interesting periods of my flying career. At about the same time I was appointed PA to the Commandant, Air Commodore 'Mark' Selway, but as this was a part-time appointment I was able to continue instructing on the Meteor. The Commandant had been one of the pre-war CFS formation aerobatic pilots and one day a photograph arrived in my in tray. It was of the pre-war team, flying Tutors with the leader inverted, at a Hendon air display. There was no note attached to the photo, but the Commandant had simply written on it: 'Re-do Meteors'. So we did.

I had always been enthusiastic with a camera so I asked if I could fly the MOD chief photographer, Mike Chase. He produced a photograph in March 1952 which hit the world's press because it was the first time this formation had

'Re-do Meteors!' Avro Tutors of the pre-War CFS display team.

CFS Meteors flying the 'Inverted Leader' formation. This was the first time it had been done with jet aircraft.

been attempted with jet aircraft. The problem was that Meteors were only cleared to fly inverted for 15 seconds, so once the leader had turned his aircraft upside down we only had 15 seconds for me and the other two to get into position and for the photographer to take his picture. In fact we found the engines would keep going for much longer than 15 seconds if full power was not used, but I was subsequently told that this did not do the oil pressure much good. Our flight commander, Caryl Gordon, went one better by leading the four Meteors with himself inverted and even led the team in the first half of a loop in this configuration.

Janusz Zurakowski, the delightful Polish Gloster chief test pilot, astonished his audience at an SBAC display at Farnborough in 1951 when he did his famous cartwheel. He would pull up to the vertical as if to do a stall turn, but would complete one and a half complete rotations to finish up pointing straight down. The next week, Meteor pilots all over the RAF were attempting this manoeuvre, but the best we could do was to complete one full rotation – rather than one and a half – and therefore finish pointing upwards, but going downhill backwards. This did not do the aircraft much good and rivets started popping all over the place, so we were quickly banned from attempting the cartwheel. The reason why Jan was successful was because he was flying Gloster's private venture Ground Attack Fighter, known as the GAF. This was finished in a

Caryl Gordon, inverted, leads the CFS Meteors in a loop.

dramatic crimson colour and was fitted with tip tanks full of fuel. The extra weight at the wing tips gave him the momentum to continue the extra half turn.

In 1953 Flight Lieutenant Les Titmus led a formation aerobatic team and a series of very fine photographs were taken by Russell Adams, the chief photographer of the Gloster Aircraft Company. I flew Russell on all the sorties,

The CFS Aerobatic Team over the Gloucestershire countryside. Russell Adams

my aim being to try and position the photographer so that he could clearly see all the aircraft. I personally felt that air-to-air pictures look better when taken alongside the target aircraft, or even ahead of them, but preferably not behind. This could mean that I sometimes had to fly formation aerobatics looking backwards, but curiously enough it is not as difficult as it sounds – a bit like riding a bicycle slightly ahead of someone else by looking back at the other bike. It was a joy to fly with Russell because he was a true enthusiast and knew exactly what he wanted. Sadly he died in 2000, but Tim Kershaw has written a marvellous book about him called 'Jet Age Photographer' and this contains the best of Russell's pictures.

I had the pleasure of flying solo aerobatics in a number of air displays with the Meteor. At that time CFS pilots had few restrictions and I was allowed to fly as low as I liked. I was able to start my display by arriving at 400 knots, upside down, at 200 ft above the ground; much of the rest of the display would also be inverted. At that period in the early 1950s we had no g limits laid down and no accelerometers to record the g loading. It is therefore hardly surprising that quite a few Meteors broke up in the air. I am sure we used to over-stress the aircraft because we did not know then what we know now about metal fatigue.

Occasionally I was asked by Examining Wing to assist them when they were short staffed. I will never forget the date of 6th February 1952 when we visited RAF Syerston to carry out standardisation checks on their instructors who were also flying Meteors. On signing in after a check flight I was told The King had just died. I had no idea that he had been seriously ill and I was deeply moved; I felt as if I had just lost a member of my own family, although I had never actually met The King.

I was invited by an old school friend, Lieutenant John Robathan RN, to a guest night at Culham where he was instructing RNR officers on the Sea Fury. Towards the end of the dinner, no doubt having been suitably refreshed and with thoughts of the possibility of adding another new type to my log book, I asked if he would fly me in one of his dual-control aircraft the next morning. To my delight he

A Hunter in formation with a Blériot? The camera never lies!

agreed. The following day, after a short briefing on emergencies, he put me in the front seat and off we went. At the time the Sea Fury was one of the fastest piston single-engine fighters in the world, powered by the huge 2,480 hp Bristol Centaurus engine giving it a top speed of 460 mph. We explored the aerobatic capabilities of this fine powerful fighter and then he demonstrated how to do a dummy deck landing. I was full of admiration for the way naval pilots carry out this procedure and it was exciting to watch how John flew the last few hundred feet very accurately and very close to the stall. We then did a few roller landings before taxying in. To my amazement he then got out and said, 'Off you go' (or words to that effect), and that fifteen minute solo remains one of my most treasured aviation memories because being allowed to fly that magnificent aircraft by myself was a complete surprise. I had not even read the pilot's notes – the instruction manual – so if I had bent his aeroplane he would undoubtedly have been in deep trouble.

We had in our museum at Little Rissington a very fine model of a Blériot, the type that first flew across the Channel in 1909. As a bit of a joke I arranged with our station photographer to cook up a picture of the Blériot in formation with a Hunter, an easy task with today's digital photography, but not so easy then. *Flight* magazine published the picture and it was amazing how many people thought it was genuine.

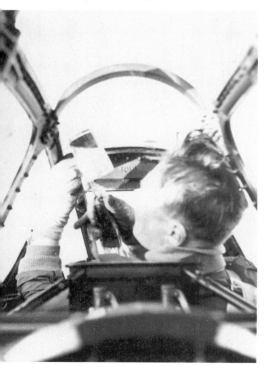

Whilst on the subject of photography, Johnny Price, another Meteor instructor, and I decided to take a photograph of a glass of Coke being poured upwards. I was to fly the aircraft from the back seat and take the photograph while flying the aircraft with the other hand upside down. All went well until we tried to turn the right way up. The trouble was that I rolled one way and he turned the glass full of Coke the other. At the moment of zero g there was a globulous lump of Coke floating around the cockpit which then splashed all over the place – not very clever.

Six months after arriving on the staff at CFS I managed to obtain the coveted A1 flying instructor's category. I was then

As seen from the rear seat of a Meteor Mk 7. Pouring a glass of Coke upwards?

Pat Rooney's cartoon drawn at Little Rissington in 1951. Pat Rooney

twenty-five years old and I was told that I was the youngest A1 in the RAF at that time, an achievement of which I am very proud. It was shortly after that when I moved to the 'Type Flight' to instruct on the Meteor, but after two and a half years as a flying instructor at CFS I felt it was time to move on and to try and return to operational flying.

Chapter 5

Air Racing

Air racing has a long and distinguished history which is well documented in the interesting website of the Society of Air Racing Historians: *www.airrace.com*. The first air race was held at Reims in 1909 and was won by the American, Glen Curtiss, in an aircraft which he had designed and built himself, and had flown at a speed of 47 mph. The following year a race was held near Los Angeles. By then air racing had helped to introduce the public at large, on both sides of the Atlantic, to aviation at a time when the construction of aircraft, the training of pilots and general air mindedness was taking hold.

The first cross-country race was sponsored by the *Daily Mail* for a first prize of £10,000. It was held in Britain in 1910 and flown from London to Manchester. The description of that race appears to be very similar to the marvellous air race shown in *Those Magnificent Men in their Flying Machines* – the only film I have seen six times.

The first handicapped air race was held in 1912 at Hendon which became the venue for a series of famous air displays in the 1920s and 1930s. Apart from the war years, handicap races have been held annually in England ever since.

The Frenchman, Jacques Schneider, was an enthusiastic supporter of seaplanes and introduced a series of races aimed at stimulating their technical development. Teams were to be organized by the aero club of the countries entering the race and any club winning three races in five years would keep the cup. Winning countries hosted the race for the following year. The first race was held at Monaco in 1913 and Britain's Royal Aero Club won in 1914 and again in 1922. By 1927 the Air Ministry considered the prestige gained by winning the race was so significant that it formed the RAF High Speed Flight for each of the next three races, the teams consisting mainly of men who had made their mark at the Central Flying School.

The 1927 race was held at Venice when two Supermarine S5s, designed by R.J. Mitchell, were entered and came 1st and 2nd, the winner being Flight

Lieutenant Sydney Webster who won at a speed of 282 mph. After that race Jacques Schneider decided to hold the race every other year. Mitchell's superb series of seaplanes won again in 1929 with Henry Waghorn flying the S6 at a speed of 329 mph, Flight Lieutenant d'Arcy Greig coming third in the old S5. Flight Lieutenant 'Batchy' Atcherley would have won the race at a speed of 332 mph had he not been disqualified for missing a pylon.

At this stage the British government withdrew its support and the 1931 entry was only possible through the generosity of Lady Houston who donated £100,000 for the development of the S6b. Flight Lieutenant John Boothman then won the trophy outright for Britain at a speed of 340 mph. Two weeks later, in the same aircraft, George Stainforth became the first man to fly at 400 mph when he broke the world air speed record at 407 mph.

As is now well known, Reginald Mitchell went on to design the wonderful Spitfire. Many of us feel that if an aircraft looks good it is good – a saying that is, of course, a generalization, but it is surprising how often it is right. It is certainly right in the case of the Spitfire. The winning S6B can be seen in the Science Museum and the Schneider Trophy is displayed in the Royal Aero Club.

R.J. Mitchell's Supermarine S6B which won the 1931 Schneider Trophy for Great Britain is now in the Science Museum. Science Museum/Science and Technology Picture Library

Each September most RAF stations hold annual Battle of Britain cocktail parties to which our civilian friends in the locality are invited. At the 1951 party at Little Rissington I met Lord and Lady Sherborne – Charles and Joan – who lived about 5 miles from the airfield. I had a fascinating conversation about their time as ferry pilots with the Air Transport Auxiliary during the War. Although Charles was a pilot, he had not joined the RAF because he only had one arm, but still managed to ferry Spitfires, amongst other aircraft. Joan currently owned a Vega Gull which she kept at Kidlington about 30 miles away, and apart from the distance, her main concern was the high hangarage fees which she had to pay. At that time RAF pilots were allowed to keep aircraft, free of charge, on their stations provided space was available in a hangar, and since I was reasonably sure we had room at Little Rissington, I offered to look after the Vega Gull for her.

The Percival Vega Gull was a delightful four-seat touring aircraft of the same parentage as the Mew Gull which had fascinated me as a boy. A military version, the Proctor, was produced during the War for communication duties. After a short time, as a 'thank you' for looking after her aircraft, Joan said, 'Would you like to enter the Vega in the King's Cup Air Race?' It is not difficult to imagine what my answer was because I realized I would then be able to achieve one of my boyhood ambitions. I was newly married and had little spare cash at the time (what's new?) so I then had to set about trying to get some sponsorship. I managed to persuade Shell to give me the fuel for the race and some practice, while De Havilland at Hatfield agreed to give the engine a top overhaul. The latter was important because the race is a handicap race, and the handicappers calculate your speed on the basis that it is a standard aircraft in perfect condition. If you make any modifications to make it go faster you have to declare them on the entry form and your handicap is then adjusted accordingly. Unfortunately they don't make corresponding allowances for clapped-out aircraft.

The King's Cup was presented by George V and was first flown in 1922 from Croydon. It is still being flown each year and has become the longest running major air race in the world. Before the War civil aircraft were as fast, if not faster than the military aircraft of the period, consequently the King's Cup had a national following not unlike that of Formula One motor racing today. *The Times* would list all the entrants and their expected speeds, and give details of the pilots and aircraft, all of which I used to study with great enthusiasm as a small boy.

The 1952 race was to be held at Newcastle Airport and the Commandant agreed that I could enter the Vega Gull as a CFS entry, so we painted the CFS crest on the engine cowling. I contacted Air Commodore Allen Wheeler, who was then Commandant at the experimental establishment at Boscombe Down, to seek his advice about air racing in general. I did not know him, but I knew of his reputation as a light aircraft enthusiast and an experienced air racer. He gave me some excellent advice along the following lines:

- Prepare the aircraft as far as possible as if it was new. The handicappers will inspect the aircraft in detail and compare it with what you have written on the entry form. If you win they will also inspect it after the race to make sure there has been no cheating.
- Navigation must be spot on. If you wander off course you will lose time.
- Turns must be as close as possible to the pylons, but if you clip the corner you will be disqualified. For safety reasons you must not climb or dive during a turn.
- Fly as low as possible into wind where the wind is least strong and then climb to about 200 ft downwind to gain the maximum benefit.

The race was to be flown over four laps round a course with four turning points, each lap being about 32 miles. I did several practice laps at about 1,000 ft in an Anson a week or so before the race to memorise the details of the course in case the visibility was poor on the day. We were given the opportunity to fly several practice laps the day before the race and were given our handicap times shortly before the start; I thought mine was very fair. Shortly after the event I wrote an article to record my impressions at the time:

I glanced at my watch; eight minutes to go before we were to be flagged away. Two Tiger Moths and the Avro Cadet had passed overhead and were already on their second lap and there were still six

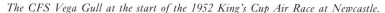

The CFS Vega Gull at the start of the 1952 King's Cup Air Race at Newcastle.

others to take off before me. Why couldn't I fly a nice slow aeroplane, I thought, and avoid all this expenditure of nervous energy. 'Can you start up now please' shouted one of the marshals. 'Can I stay another couple of minutes, I have no oil cooler and she gets a bit hot? No? Oh very well!' The next worry is will she start? One push of the button and she fired first go, I saw satisfied smiles from my crew, Ian Scott and my brother Dick, who were standing by my wing tips. A moment or two later we were marshalled forward to fill the gap of the last competitor away. The starter held up two fingers which I hoped meant two minutes to go (this I checked with my watch and I found it to be so). The last Proctor had been flagged away and beside me was Ron Paine's beautifully polished Miles Hawk Speed Six which was not due off for some time.

Whilst I was noting all this I suddenly realised the starter's flag was up which meant I had ten seconds to go, so I opened up the throttle as far as I could against the brakes (no point in checking the magneto switches for fear of frightening myself) and as the flag was whipped down: throttle fully forward, brakes off, tail up and the event we had looked forward to for so long had actually arrived.

Shortly after crossing the airfield boundary lay the first turning point of nearly 180° which then set us off on the first leg towards St Mary's Lighthouse. This turn safely negotiated we settled down on our first leg which we flew at about 200 ft to get the most out of the tail wind. There was no difficulty in staying on course because one kept an enormous slag heap slightly to the left of track until we could see the lighthouse dead ahead. It was interesting to watch the turning techniques of the experts. Some rolled rapidly into the turn, hauled the aircraft round and rolled out rapidly. This looked impressive, but it did result in a loss of speed. Others took a more gentle approach to avoid losing too much speed; I had no option but to take the latter course because the Vega's ailerons were fantastically heavy at full speed and it was hard work to roll at all. The second leg was a straight forward run over the sea as low as one dare, but the third was more difficult being a climb of some 500 ft over coal mining country. The fourth leg led straight towards the airfield and again meant a few more minutes of glorious legal low flying.

All the four legs were about eight miles long and took the Vega about three minutes to complete, but the Vampire, flown by test pilot John Wilson, only took four minutes to complete the whole lap. Since the handicappers had aimed to have us all cross the finishing line at the same time, there was not much excitement until the third lap when we began to bunch up a little and we could see it was going to be an exciting finish. As I was starting the last lap I noticed that all the other aircraft except the Vampire had taken off. It subsequently overtook me four times before finishing three places in front of me.

It was on the third lap that I hit one of the biggest bumps that I had ever experienced as I came round the lee side of a wood. My head hit the roof and there was a most alarming noise from the wing like a revolver shot. However, we were all in one piece so we pressed on. Inspection later revealed a flabby piece of canvas which seemed to have absorbed much of the shock. I now feel confident to fly the Vega through the most violent of storms (or do I?).

The last leg was incredibly exciting. We were overtaken by several others, but we on the other hand had overtaken even more. As the finishing line loomed ahead I saw one of the two Miles Messengers just in front, but I failed to catch it before the end of the race. In fact we started 16th out of 23 and finished 11th at an average speed of 155 mph. The Vampire had flown at 460 mph. After nearly an hour flying at full throttle I checked the oil after landing and as I lifted the filler cap there was a puff of blue smoke! The next day the engine ran sweeter than ever and a previous 'mag drop' had disappeared.

On looking back, an air race seems to be a series of individual battles; you win one and then sort out the next fellow. All the competitors seemed incredibly friendly and would give you a cheery wave as they overtook you. They helped one another on the ground with advice on flying the race and even assistance in preparing aircraft. There was no feeling of cut-throat competition – just everyone out for a good sporting race.

This was written over half a century ago, but the memory is as vivid as ever. The achievement of my boyhood ambition was every bit as exciting as I had hoped it would be. A few years later I was to get another chance to fly in the King's Cup.

Chapter 6
Back to the Front Line

Towards the end of my tour as a CFS instructor I applied to join No. 2 Squadron in Germany equipped with Supermarine Swifts in the fighter reconnaissance role. It was commanded by Squadron Leader Bob Weighill who had been my squadron commander at Cranwell when I was instructing. He said he would be willing to apply for me, but he pointed out that although I was due to become a flight commander, it would not be possible on 2 Squadron because both positions were already filled. I therefore applied to join No. 98 Squadron, then based at Fassberg and flying the De Havilland Venom Mk 1. The Squadron was commanded by Squadron Leader John Smith-Carington who had been with me on the same course at the Central Flying School five years earlier. He agreed to apply for me, but said I would have to wait my turn to become a flight commander because a post would not become available for a few months. I gladly accepted this situation and was duly posted to Fassberg in January 1954 after attending the Operational Conversion Unit on Vampires at Chivenor.

The RAF's 2nd Tactical Air Force (2nd TAF) had fought in Germany early in 1945 and, after Germany surrendered in May, the RAF took on the new role of occupying and disarming a defeated country. 2nd TAF then became BAFO, the British Air Force of Occupation, in July. Germany had already been divided into zones, the western border of the Russian Zone becoming the border between East and West Germany; the United States, Britain and France having the other three zones. Berlin was in the Russian Zone and three air corridors joined the city to the American and British Zones. Disputes between the Soviet Union and the Western democracies, particularly over the Soviet takeover of Eastern European states, led Winston Churchill to say that 'From Stettin in the Baltic to Trieste in the Adriatic, an iron curtain has descended across the Continent. Behind that line lie all the capitals of Central and Eastern Europe.' This was at a speech to Westminster College, Fulton, Missouri in March 1946. Add to this Stalin's rhetoric declaring that war was an inevitable consequence of the conflict between communism and capitalist

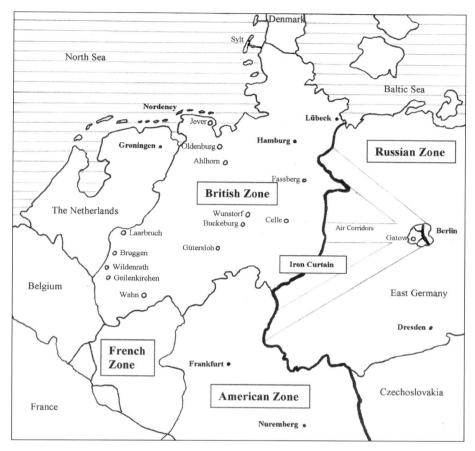

The Allied Zones in Germany after the Second World War. Berlin itself was divided into the four sectors.

imperialism, and the 'Cold War' was born. This became a period when both sides genuinely believed that the other was the potential aggressor. Both East and West had nuclear weapons as a deterrent, thus creating a nuclear stalemate.

Powerful Western armed forces were thus established in Germany to deter any possible aggression, but if that deterrence failed, then those forces had to be strong enough to be able to repel an attack. RAF bomber, reconnaissance and fighter squadrons were therefore maintained in the British Zone; 98 Squadron was one of these. A glance at the map shows that there were a large number of RAF bases in our Zone, thus making a significant contribution to the overall deterrent.

In 1948 the Russians engineered a communist takeover in Czechoslovakia and in April of that year the British Chiefs of Staff decided that future plans were to be based on the assumption that Russia was the potential enemy. In June the Russians closed the entire road, rail and water routes linking West

Berlin – the three sectors of which were controlled by Britain, France and the USA – with the three zones in West Germany. For the Allies to have accepted this blockade as a fait accompli would have meant the loss of Berlin as a free city in their foothold in East Germany. The only way in which two million West Berliners could be kept alive was to ferry food, coal and raw materials in by air using the three air corridors. The Russians made no attempt to block these and the operation became known as 'The Berlin Air Lift'. At its height some 8,000 tons of supplies were being delivered daily with British, French and American aircraft arriving every three minutes in good weather and five minutes in bad. This lasted until May 1949 when the Russian blockade was lifted. A month earlier the North Atlantic Treaty had been signed, Article 5 of which declared that an attack on one of the members would be considered an attack on them all. Fassberg was one of the major airfields used during the Berlin Air Lift.

We were envious of the Americans who were based in their Zone in the south because it seemed to us that they occupied a far pleasanter part of the country than ours in the north which tended to be flat and uninteresting. At the time I had a theory that people who lived in mountainous areas were much more interesting than those who lived on the level, and I compared favourably, probably quite unjustly, the Bavarians and their cheerful music (and beer drinking) in the south to those I was living amongst in the north.

By the time I arrived at Fassberg BAOR had already, in 1951, resumed its earlier title of 2nd TAF and this title remained until 1959 when the Command was once again renamed, this time as 'RAF Germany'. Gradually the Luftwaffe had been able to take over our stations and the last RAF aircraft, a Tornado, was flown out of RAF Brüggen in 2001.

Fassberg was a magnificent ex-Luftwaffe base that the Allies never found until towards the end of the War. It was well camouflaged in a large forested area about 80 km south-east of Hamburg and very close to the notorious concentration camp at Belsen. It was also quite close to the Iron Curtain and great care had to be taken not to fly accidentally over the border because that tended to upset the Russians and invariably resulted in formal diplomatic complaints.

As part of the deterrent we took our turn with other stations to form 'Battle Flights'. During daylight hours four aircraft would form the Battle Flight by being fully armed with the pilots of a pair of aircraft sitting in their cockpits at immediate readiness, lined up at the end of the runway ready to intercept any unidentified aircraft seen on radar to be entering our Zone. Pilots would rotate every two hours.

There were two other Venom squadrons at Fassberg: Nos 14 and 118. Whilst each squadron had its own distinctive spirit, the morale of the station as a whole was exceptionally high and although we flew hard we also played hard.

The Venom was a good aircraft and was pleasant to fly; it performed like a hotted up Vampire and in particular it had a relatively good high-altitude performance. Our role was DF/GA – Day Fighter and Ground Attack. In the ground-attack role we liaised closely with the Army and cooperated with them on frequent exercises. So that we understood each other as best as we could we used to invite army officers to spend a few days with us and to fly in the two-seat Vampire which we used for training and the checking of our own pilots. In turn some of us volunteered to spend a few days with the Army.

In 1954 I asked if I could spend a week with the Royal Welch Fusiliers who were based to the north of us at Lüneburg. Their commanding officer said that he would be glad to have me, but that they were very busy at the time training for the Korean War and that, if I wanted to come, I would have to do a job of work. Of course I agreed, but was rather surprised to find that I had been appointed as a platoon commander for the week. The troops accepted the situation in very good heart and I had excellent guidance and support from their platoon sergeant. On our last day, a Saturday, I was marching up and down with two other junior officers waiting to go on parade when one of them said, 'How have you enjoyed your week with us?' I replied that I had enjoyed it immensely, but that I now knew that I could never make a soldier (I had always known that, but I didn't admit it). 'Why ever not?' one of them asked, 'You've done alright with us.' I pointed out that although I had enjoyed the week, I could never actually enjoy crawling around in freezing mud whilst being shot at. To which I received the astonishing reply: 'But surely you don't actually enjoy flying those things do you?' It hadn't occurred to them that pilots in the RAF thoroughly enjoy their flying. Indeed I believe it would be very difficult to become a pilot if you were not enthusiastic about the role. I would even go so far as to say that it would be difficult to do anything in life really well unless your heart is in it and you really enjoyed the work.

Having said that, I was full of admiration for the qualities shown by the junior officers in the Army towards their men. From Day 1 they are taught to be good 'officers', and as infantrymen they are put in charge of thirty or so men as soon as they join their regiment. They learn how to deal with some pretty tough characters and how to turn them into good soldiers whilst at the same time being concerned about their welfare. By contrast, in the RAF, our primary concern when we first graduate to a squadron is to be busy learning how to operate our aircraft, the airmen who service our aircraft being commanded, not by the pilots, but by their engineering officers. It is therefore quite possible for an RAF pilot not to have commanded airmen directly until he becomes quite senior, possibly not even until he becomes a group captain station commander. This might account for a remark made to me when I was on my first squadron. I was a newly commissioned pilot officer driving past Pocklington in Yorkshire when I stopped outside the army base there to pick up an airman in uniform who was thumbing a lift to York. I was in civilian clothes and there was nothing to suggest I was in the RAF. I was intrigued to find out why an airman was working on an army base so we got into conversation. It seemed he was a signals specialist who was on a course with the army signallers, so I asked him what he thought of the young army officers who were looking after him. He said he was full of admiration for the way they would come into their barrack huts and chat over any problems, helping wherever they could. 'What do you think of RAF officers then?' I asked, silently hoping to be flattered. That turned out to be a silly thing to have asked because he replied, 'Between you and me, sir, they're a lot of spivs!' I hoped he was wrong, but I understood the point he was making and, as the years rolled by, I tried not to forget that lesson.

The social life at the time in Germany was about as good as it gets. There were many squadron parties and the bar in the Mess was invariably full. TGIF (Thank God It's Friday) parties were the norm and always well supported. No doubt we drank more of the excellent German beer than we should have done, but there was never the present tendency towards binge drinking and I never remember drink being the cause of any unpleasantness. I can't remember how it began, but 98 used to attend parties in our squadron uniforms – bowler hats and smart grey suits! What a contrast to the way we all dress today.

Six months after joining 98 Squadron I became a flight commander. I tried hard to inject enthusiasm and fun into the training of the pilots, because, as mentioned earlier, I didn't believe they could do their job properly if they didn't enjoy it. This obviously paid off because one night in the bar, doubtless after quite a few jars of German beer, one of my officers came up to me and thanked me for giving him back his enthusiasm for flying.

98 Squadron in party mode. L to R: Eddie McCullagh, JS, Curly Hirst, Be Be Sharman, Ken Williams, Dave Sawyer, Bodger Edwards, Dave Young.

I was keen to fulfil my second ambition of owning a Mercedes, but unfortunately the sports cars I was interested in were extremely rare, although pre-war saloon cars were obtainable. I managed to buy a 1938 Mercedes 230 which had been a German Army staff car and which had survived the War. It was in remarkably good condition, apart from the fact that it seemed to consume more oil than petrol, it was built like a tank and had independent suspension on all four wheels. It cost me £85 and I was very proud of my new possession.

After three months or so we were allocated a married quarter. My wife then flew out from UK with our two young daughters to join me and I met them at Hamburg with the car I had just bought, hoping fervently that it would not break down on the way to the airport. We were delighted with our ex-Luftwaffe officer's married quarter; it had double glazing and central heating which was a good thing because the temperature would drop to around zero farenheit in the winter. We take these things for granted now, but at that time double glazing was virtually unknown at home and few of our UK married quarters were centrally heated.

There were insufficient quarters at Fassberg for all the married officers to be accompanied by their wives. Since, at that time, we were not able to hire local German accommodation, there were many unaccompanied officers living in the Mess in addition to the single officers. We knew the German staff made much of Christmas so we decided to close the Mess on Christmas Day in 1955 so that the staff could all go home. Those of us in married quarters then invited all the officers who were living in the Mess to our homes for the day, but there was a slight complication to this seemingly simple celebration. It is an old custom that, on Christmas Day, the officers serve the airmen their traditional Christmas lunch in the Airmen's Mess. This is invariably followed by an invitation from the senior NCOs to invite the officers to the Sergeant's Mess for a Christmas drink. The consequence of all this was that we seldom arrived home for our own Christmas lunch until about 4 pm. Thankfully, our gallant wives somehow managed to cope with this difficult situation. In appreciation of what we did for those officers living in the Mess, they, in turn, invited all the married officers and their wives to a ladies guest night just after Christmas. Although this dinner was the usual formal occasion, it was the first time any of us could remember ladies being invited to a guest night. It was tremendously successful and is now common practice, but it was an innovation at that time.

I have to admit that times were hard then for the Germans, although dramatic improvements had already been made compared to the immediate aftermath of the War. When I visited Lübeck in 1946 the Deutschmark was almost worthless and I remember being followed by children wherever we went, waiting to pick up fag ends because tobacco had become a form of currency. Twenty cigarettes would buy a good dinner in a restaurant. Even eight years later we would see women following the lorries delivering coal to the married quarters, hoping to pick up a few lumps which might fall out of the bags. On the other hand, conditions for the occupying forces were very good. As a flight lieutenant we were entitled to a full-time housekeeper, a full-time living-in nanny for the children – a very nice young German girl called Irma – a part-time gardener and also a part-time boilerman to stoke our central heating boiler twice daily. Needless to say, with a young family at that time we particularly appreciated the domestic help. Petrol was rationed, but the allowance was adequate and it was cheap for the Forces.

We had a good riding stable on the station with several horses and a full-time German groom. My wife and I spent many happy hours riding in the forest of Örrel which bordered the airfield. It was not long before I was found out and made officer in charge of the stables, but this time it was doing something which I thoroughly enjoyed, and perhaps more importantly, it was something we could do together.

At about the same time as I was appointed a flight commander, Fassberg was tasked with carrying out trials and demonstrations of the use of napalm. I was one of two pilots selected for this interesting activity. Napalm is jellied petrol which was carried in fuel tanks slung beneath the wing (I think they were 100-gallon tanks) and which could be jettisoned. The effect viewed from the ground was dramatic and to some, quite frightening. We used a Vampire Mk 5 and most of the trials and demonstrations were carried out on the range at Fassberg. The technique was to approach the target at 360 knots at a height of only 20 ft which itself was quite exciting. There was no bomb sight of any kind and we dropped the 'bomb' by eye, simply pulling the fuel tank jettison lever

Dropping Napalm from a Vampire on the Fassberg Range.

when we judged the moment was right. After a little practice we were able to achieve direct hits on most occasions. Our practices were usually carried out with water in the tanks, but even that was quite impressive. I remember one of those demonstrations very clearly when I flew from Fassberg to Tangmere, and from there to take part in a 'Firepower Demonstration' on Salisbury Plain. These demonstrations were regularly held to show off the various military and air force weapons the UK produced, consequently the large audiences included foreign senior officers together with their military attachés. We had a rehearsal the day before using water and just after releasing the 'bomb' I flew over the top of the target tank and saw, out of the corner of my eye, two pressmen running away. They had been hiding behind the far side of the tank hoping to get a good picture, but they must have got more than they bargained for – imagine the noise of a 100-gallon fuel tank hitting a very solid object at 360 knots only feet away. I had no idea whether I had hit the target, or whether I had overshot it and perhaps killed the pressmen, so I explained what I had seen on the R/T and asked whether the two idiots were safe. Thankfully they were because I had achieved a direct hit, but I don't suppose they ever tried that trick again. I have never been particularly fond of the gentlemen of the press, but I have never considered trying to kill them.

On my return from Tangmere, the day after the demonstration, the weather over Germany was very poor, and as I started my descent I asked for a bearing to Fassberg as I was not sure where I was – this is given by an operator on the ground who can tell the direction of the radio transmission from the aircraft. After a number of bearings had been transmitted I became suspicious because I felt certain that I must have passed over the top of Fassberg and was therefore heading for the Russian Zone. After checking, the operator admitted he had been giving me reciprocal bearings, in other words I was going in the opposite direction to that intended. After landing we calculated that I must have been at least 20 miles into the Russian Zone and I therefore waited for the inevitable diplomatic complaint. It never arrived because we learnt later from intelligence sources that the Russian radar was unserviceable on that day.

We enjoyed flying the Venom, but it did have its problems when it first came into service in 1953 and these are well documented in David Watkins' excellent book *Venom*. He tells of how Sam D'Arcy of 14 Squadron ejected in March 1954 when a wing broke off as he was pulling out of a practice dive-bombing attack on the Fassberg range. He was so low when he ejected that his parachute had only just deployed as he hit the ground. I met him in the bar very shortly after the incident – his face was cut and bruised because there was no time for him to jettison the canopy before ejection. He therefore had to eject through it – hence the battering on his face. Luckily his injuries were superficial and he was enjoying his well deserved drink. There had been several previous accidents when the wings failed and until the aircraft were modified they had red bands painted on the wings to remind pilots to limit the g forces. We also had a

Venom Mk 1s of 98 Squadron. Brian Sharman

number of inexplicable fires in the air and several pilots were killed when attempting forced landings because the fires had burnt through the elevator control cables. Pilots were therefore given strict orders to eject if they had a fire and not to attempt a forced landing, even if the fire appeared to be out.

In October 1954 one of the pilots on my flight, George Schofield, was killed when he attempted to land after a fire. Four days later on 1st November, in beautiful weather, I was at the top of a loop at 10,000 ft directly over Fassberg when I decided to hold the aircraft inverted for a few moments before rolling level. Whilst still inverted there was a bang, the fire warning light came on and the cockpit filled with smoke. After completing the fire drill, which obviously included shutting down the engine, I prepared myself for a forced landing on the airfield which I could see clearly beneath me. I knew I was under orders to eject, but I was very conscious of George's accident and I was overcome by a conviction that this had happened to me, his flight commander, so that the riddle of the fires could be solved. I decided to land wheels up on the grass by the side of the runway so that I would be able to get out of the aircraft quickly if needs be. We had all regularly practised forced landings and, with height to spare and perfect weather, I had no difficulty in positioning myself to land alongside the runway in use. I had never landed wheels up before and was surprised how gentle it was. The moment I came to a halt the fire engines were alongside and, since there was no obvious sign of the fire still burning, I prevented the fire crews from smothering the engine in foam in case this destroyed valuable evidence. The first thing I did when I got back to our hangar was to brief the other pilots in the crew room what had happened and to emphasize that under no circumstances were they to attempt to land after a fire – they *must* eject. Shortly after that the Wing Commander Flying entered the crew room and gave me a severe ticking off, and then added, 'But well done!' It appeared that he had also been airborne at the time and heard what was happening over the R/T. He knew he should have ordered me to eject, but I gather he sensed what I was trying to do and kept quiet. The Board of Inquiry thought the fact that the fire started whilst I was inverted might be significant so they rigged up a complete Venom fuel system upside down in a hangar and they did indeed solve the problem. I have to admit that for the first few sorties after that incident my eyes tended to concentrate on the fire warning light and it took me a month or so before I was able to relax in the cockpit. For this incident I was subsequently awarded the Air Force Cross.

Venoms were not the only aircraft that tended to catch fire. The Americans were flying F84 Thunderstreaks in their zone to the south and the story was around that, if these aircraft caught fire, you had only four seconds in which to eject before the whole lot exploded. One of the aircraft in a formation caught fire and one of the other pilots shouted on the R/T, 'Hank, you're on fire', whereupon four Hanks throughout the zone ejected! I don't know how true the story was, but it was often used as an example of why strict R/T discipline is essential. If the pilot's callsign had been used rather than his first name, three aircraft would have been saved.

Shortly before my Venom fire I fell asleep at the wheel of our Mercedes one night returning from dinner with an old friend at the Officers' Club at Celle. The road went round a corner at Uelzen, but unfortunately I went straight on. Despite the fact that we broke a telephone pole in two, the damage to my tank-like Mercedes was not severe, but the damage to my wife was. This was before the advent of seat belts and she was thrown forward, her face hitting a sharp knob which was used to open the windscreen. She cracked a collar bone, but much more seriously fractured her cheek bone in several places, the knob missing her eye by a fraction of an inch. If seat belts had been introduced at that time she would have been uninjured. On the other hand I have always felt that had the car been of a more modern flimsy construction, we might both have had serious injuries. In those days no countries had drink and drive laws and I was almost certainly over the present day limit. It's a sad fact that few of us serving in Germany at that time completed our tours without having some sort of road accident. I subsequently sold the damaged car for £90 – having only paid £85 for it in the first place, it wasn't a bad deal.

In the spring of 1955 I was sent on the Day Fighter Leaders Course at West Raynham. This was an excellent two month course learning, as the name implies, how to be a fighter leader both in air defence and ground attack roles. Most significantly to me the course flew the new Hunters which had only come into service the year before. These were Mk 1 Hunters which were a great advance over the Venoms, and whilst they were a delight to fly, they were somewhat limited on fuel – after forty minutes at low level one was really starting to get worried. The course taught us how to operate the aircraft to its limit, so much so that at the end of one sortie one of the members on our course ran out of fuel whilst taxying back in. We were trained how to plan an attack on a ground target leading up to twelve aircraft, aiming to be on target plus or minus fifteen seconds. We only had twenty minutes to work out the plan and prepare maps and to brief the other pilots before rushing to our Hunters to take off. We were also taught how to control a squadron in the air when attacking hostile aircraft; it is particularly difficult to control the situation when aircraft appear to be all over the sky. Above all, we learnt how to get the best out of our wonderful new Hunters.

When I returned to 98 Squadron after the DFLS course, the squadron had by then moved to Jever, not far from Wilhelmshaven in the north of Germany, and had re-equipped with Hunter Mk 4s. The Hunter could exceed the speed of sound in a dive, but not in level flight. It was therefore classed a 'transonic' rather than 'supersonic'. We found that four aircraft diving together through the sound barrier, and pointing at the airfield, could make a dramatic multiple sonic boom on the ground. Not surprisingly those on the ground were not amused and this practice was rapidly prohibited.

Jever was in a flat and uninteresting area of Germany not far from the North Sea, the air was often damp and many of the children including ours had ear problems. We sometimes took the children with Irma to the sea for the day at Shillig, the nearest sandy beach. Irma had moved with us from Fassberg and the first time she saw the sea she asked, 'What are those funny white things?' She had never before seen the sea, let alone white horses.

Although the War had ended five years before there was very little socializing between us, yet on the whole our relationships with the German population were good, although things appeared to be different in Holland, or so I discovered to my embarrassment. Sometimes we would treat ourselves to a day's shopping over the border, usually at Groningen, and on one occasion I stopped to fill up with petrol. I had not learnt to speak German properly, but I knew enough to be able to shop or to ask the way. Without thinking, I spoke

The author as a happy flight commander with a Hunter of 98 Squadron. Brian Sharman

in German and said, 'Zwanzig litre bitte.' Whereupon an angry Dutch garage owner, recognizing us as British, said in English, 'Don't you use that language in my country.' I realized then that there was still no love lost between the two nations.

No. 98 Squadron at Jever with Elspeth their mascot. Brian Sharman

We had a station farm at Jever which provided us with fresh food and vegetables. We adopted a very beautiful mascot named Elspeth. Elspeth was a pig. She was a great supporter of the squadron and would appear on major occasions.

One of the other squadrons at Jever, No. 93, was operating the North American Mk 4 F86 Sabre. Ever anxious to get my hands on a new type I persuaded their squadron commander to let me fly one of his aircraft. My main impression of this excellent machine was the huge cockpit. Cockpits of British fighter aircraft tended to be cosy with everything close at hand, but the Sabre's cockpit seemed massive compared to anything I had been used to before. The Sabre, incidentally, was very successful in Korea in combating the MiG-15s.

At that time the six monthly promotions used to be announced the day before they were to take effect on 1st January or 1st July each year, which usually meant a move to a new unit within two or three weeks of promotion. Someone else would then have to be posted to the job you had vacated and so on, resulting in a mass of short-notice postings throughout the RAF. Station commanders often used to announce promotions at a New Year's eve ball, if there was one, resulting in much popping of champagne bottles, but the announcement of my promotion from flight lieutenant to squadron leader was certainly unusual. On 30th December 1955 I was night flying, and at one minute past midnight the Wing Commander Flying called me up on the R/T and said, 'Congratulations squadron leader!' Luckily this silly system was changed a few years later so that officers now get three months notice or so of future promotion, so that everyone has plenty of time to plan future moves. Although I was excited at my immediate future prospects, I was very sorry indeed to leave such a happy squadron as 98.

However, true to form, I was posted within a fortnight to RAF Oldenburg, near Bremen, to command No. 26 (Army Co-Operation) Squadron which had been the first in Germany to be re-equipped with the Mk 4 Hunter. I arrived on the evening of 15th January and the following morning asked the way to our hangar. There was no one to meet me so I asked the way to the CO's office and started from there – my predecessor had already left and I therefore had no handover. Luckily I had two experienced flight commanders, one of whom, John Crowley, had been a test pilot developing the Hunter at Boscombe Down. I flew with the squadron for the first time that night, a sort of mirror image of my last flight as a flight commander with 98 Squadron, which had also been at night.

26 Squadron was formed after a group of South African pilots who had learned to fly in England before the outbreak of the First World War, and who had formed a unit at Netheravon in November 1915. The origins of the squadron account for the squadron badge depicting a springbok and an Afrikaans motto: 'N Wagter in die Lug' – A Guard in the Sky. In 1953 the South African Air Force presented the squadron with a fine springbok's head and this was mounted on the wall in the CO's office behind his chair.

Neville Duke, the Hunter's test pilot, sent me a beautiful signed photograph of the prototype, WB188, which was subsequently modified to enable him to break the World Speed Record in 1963 at 727.6 mph. The photograph of Neville Duke flying the aircraft was taken by Cyril Peckham, Hawker Siddeley Aviation's chief photographer, hung in my office, but is now a treasured possession at home. This picture dramatically illustrates the belief so many of us have that if an aircraft looks right, it is right.

In the summer of 1956 we went on a three week camping holiday through Bavaria and Austria on our way to Venice. By the time we got to Vienna the temperature was 104° and a 2-litre bottle of cider had already exploded in the back of the car making a ghastly sticky mess. We had had enough of uncomfortable driving by then and decided to stay put for a week or so in a delightful camping site in the Vienna Woods, just outside the city, before returning. It proved to be good decision and we came to love Vienna. We were particularly lucky to be able to see the wonderful Lipizzaner stallions of the Spanish Riding School performing in their beautiful baroque riding hall, led by Colonel Podhajsky who had revived the School after the War. Poetry, art and music in motion seems to sum up their superb performance.

Neville Duke flying the prototype Hunter which was subsequently converted to the Mk 3 in which he won the World Air Speed Record of 727.6 mph in 1963. Cyril Peckham

Married quarters were allocated on a points basis, points being awarded for seniority, length of time married, number of children etc. and several of our young officers who had not yet gained enough points were not able to have their wives join them in Germany. Therefore, those of us lucky enough to have quarters, usually let these unaccompanied officers stay in our houses when we went on leave so that they could bring their wives out from UK for a holiday. We did just that on our camping holiday to Vienna. There must have been some misunderstanding about the date of our return because, when we arrived home after a 600-mile journey travelling through Austria and Germany, we found that our guests were not expecting us to return until the next day. We could not possibly turn them out of the house that evening, so we happily set up our tent again, this time in our own garden.

John Crowley's expertise came in very handy when we had some fairly serious problems with the Rolls Royce Avon engines of our Hunters which tended to surge at high altitude when pulling high g forces, often resulting in a flame-out. Whilst it was easy to relight the engines, it would not exactly be helpful have an engine flame-out in combat. John assured us that the engines should be able to operate correctly at high altitude and that we should press Rolls Royce and Boscombe Down to solve the problem. We were losing quite a bit of flying time with unserviceable aircraft because of these difficulties and consequently my station commander – a group captain who will remain nameless – called me to his office and said, 'Unless you can achieve more flying hours like the other squadrons I will find another squadron commander.' Although I did not express it at the time, I was furious at this comment because I knew the other squadrons were minimizing the problem by doing much of their training at low level, but I couldn't say that to the station commander. Engineers and test pilots visited us and eventually the matter was solved. This was effectively demonstrated by John Crowley leading all fourteen of the squadron's aircraft in

No. 26 Squadron's Formation Aerobatic Team painted by Bruno Albers.

a formation fly-past over the base, which happened during our camping holiday and was a very welcome surprise on my return, even if I had missed the fun myself.

Geoff Wilkinson, the senior flight commander, formed and led a formation aerobatic team which became the representative team for the 2nd TAF in Germany. I commissioned a young German artist, Bruno Albers, to paint a picture of the team which I presented to the squadron. Bruno had never flown, yet I think he successfully caught the feeling of what it is like to dance the clouds on laughter silvered wings.

I well remember briefing my squadron the day when Duncan Sandys, the Defence Minister, introduced his 1957 Statement on Defence. The then conservative government had stated that manned bombers would be replaced by ballistic missiles and that air defence would eventually be carried out by surface-to-air missiles, thus making manned aircraft virtually redundant. This led to the cancellation of the TSR2 supersonic manned bomber in 1965, while the English Electric P1, which was later named the Lightning and came into service in 1960, was to be the last manned fighter – all of which, of course, had a disastrous effect on morale throughout the RAF. Initially it also affected recruiting because parents and head teachers thought they saw no future for flying in our Service and youngsters were even discouraged from joining the Air Training Corps. How wrong Duncan Sandys was is indicated by the fact that there is little sign, nearly fifty years later, of pilots becoming redundant, although the use of unmanned aircraft is certainly on the increase as proved by their successful involvement in several recent wars. At my briefing to the squadron I stated quite firmly that I believed the Government was wrong and that manned aircraft had a solid future for years to come. It is nice occasionally to be proved right.

26 Squadron was disbanded at Oldenburg in September 1957, only to re-form a year later at Gütersloh with Hunter Mk 6s, which it flew until disbanding yet again in December 1960. In 1962 it re-formed with the twin rotor

The Springbok's head presented to No. 26 Squadron in 1953 by the South African Air Force.

Belvedere helicopter and saw sterling service in Aden during the Radfan Campaign for two and a half years before disbanding once more. It finally re-formed in 1969 at Wyton as a non-operational communications squadron, but disbanded for good on 1st April 1976. Before disbanding, the squadron tried to contact all those who had given silver, pictures and so on in order that these items could be returned to the donors rather than have them put away and forgotten in some Maintenance Unit. The picture of the formation aerobatic team was therefore returned to me. I was worried about the future of the springbok head so I asked the CO what had happened to it, whereupon I was told that it had been badly damaged and they had thrown it away. I was not amused and asked if it could be recovered so that I could collect it. This I did and found that the whole of the front of the head had been broken off so I went to our sick quarters – nowadays known as medical centres – and asked for some plaster of Paris so that I could repair the head. I was pleased with my handiwork and the scar can hardly be seen – the springbok now wears a squadron tie and is proudly displayed at my home.

Chapter 7

Grounded

Very few RAF pilots look forward to their first staff job and they certainly don't look forward to having to work in London, but the inevitable happened when I was sent to the Air Ministry – as it was then called – after 26 Squadron was disbanded in September 1957. We decided to live outside London because we wanted to bring up our three daughters in the country; I therefore had to commute daily from Haslemere where we were fortunate to be able to rent a very nice house. Despite the horrors of commuting and having to 'fly' a desk, I surprised myself by actually enjoying the work. As a squadron leader I was part of a small team in the Air Secretary's Department selecting other squadron leaders of the General Duties (GD) branch for their next appointments. Having made our selections, the candidates' names would go before an appointments board and the board would then either confirm our recommendations or tell us to think again. There were three of us in the office and I was responsible for Fighter Command and the Special Duties List (SDL). The SDL included all those interesting exchange appointments to foreign air forces, air attachés and any jobs that were not in the normal career pattern of flying and staff appointments within the Royal Air Force. I had the secondary job of being Personal Staff Officer (PSO) to the Air Secretary, an Air Marshal who was responsible for officers' careers throughout the service. This mainly involved accompanying the Air Secretary when he went on visits. The Air Secretary was also the Air Member for Personnel (AMP) on the Air Force Board.

Soon after I was appointed as his PSO, the Air Secretary, Sir Denis Barnett, decided to carry out a visit to Ceylon and Singapore. 216 Squadron of Transport Command had re-equipped with Mk 2 Comets the previous year, becoming the world's first military jet transport squadron. We were fortunate enough to travel in that wonderful aircraft and on the way home we stopped at RAF Khormaksar in Aden. That night there had been one of Aden's very rare rain showers and the runway was therefore wet when we attempted to take off the following morning. I was sitting next to a window overlooking the wing and after a few hundred yards I saw considerable quantities of water coming out of an engine vent on top of the wing. This was followed by hard braking as we came to a halt on the runway – apparently the nose wheel had gone through a large puddle and thrown water into the two inboard engines which promptly failed.

A relief Comet was flown out and we took off successfully the next day for Lyneham. The Comets were subsequently modified to ensure that the spray from the nose wheel did not enter the engines in such a disastrous fashion.

When we passed through customs at Lyneham I was surprised to see that the luggage of the airmen who had been travelling with us was being carefully searched, whilst the luggage of the senior officers was being let through without question. As we were all travelling together I found this rather embarrassing, so I asked one of the customs officers why they were doing this. He replied that the senior officers had bought things in Singapore that were clearly for their own use – such as garden furniture – whereas, in the past, some of the airmen had been caught with quantities of watches in their luggage which were obviously for resale. Having said that, I personally have always experienced a good relationship between station commanders and customs officers, because I think they know that we would come down very hard on anyone who was caught trying to cheat their way through the arrival process. I was told of a case where a number of Swiss watches were periodically on sale in shops in North Wales. The customs officers were suspicious and eventually found that the watches always appeared on the market shortly after a certain member of aircrew from Lyneham visited the area on leave. Instead of laying a trap for him they warned the station commander that they would catch him next time he returned to UK. This gave the station commander the opportunity to ensure that the problem never reoccurred. This could only have happened because there was trust on both sides.

Shortly after our visit to the Far East, Air Marshal Sir John Whitley took over as Air Secretary and AMP. He was in current flying practice on the Canberra having previously been AOC of No. 1 Group in Bomber Command, so, not surprisingly, when he decided to visit the Middle East, he flew his own Canberra. I was to be a passenger on the jump seat, but so that I could help with checks etc. I felt I ought to do a quick Canberra conversion course. I therefore managed to persuade the Operational Conversion Unit at Basssingbourn that this would be a good idea and after four dual sorties I was sent solo – another type in the log book. Apart from my one-day stop in Aden with the Comet, this was the first time I had visited the Middle East and over the next two weeks we called in to Akrotiri (Cyprus), El Adem (Libya), Khormaksar (Aden), Bahrain, Habbaniya (Iraq), Luqa (Malta) and Gibraltar. All very exciting.

I enjoyed the work in the Air Secretary's Department because we were dealing with real people in real time and, hopefully, we were being helpful. But after only nine months a strange turn of events took place.

Chapter 8

An Unusual Appointment

Whilst in the Air Secretary's Department one of the appointments I was trying to fill was that of Equerry to HRH the Duke of Edinburgh which was a general duties (aircrew) squadron leader post. I searched through the records of all the GD squadron leaders in the RAF and selected those whom I thought were the twelve best candidates. The Air Secretary then whittled this list down to a short list of four and these were submitted to Buckingham Palace. All four were rejected. I did not know how to solve this impasse because I really thought I had picked out the best possible candidates – and they had all failed. What I did not know was that my two colleagues in our office had been working on me in the meantime. Miraculously I was accepted and in 1958 I took over the job at one day's notice for a half-day handover. Thus began three and a half very happy and exciting years working for Prince Philip. I doubt even now if there is anyone who did not think that I had fixed this posting for myself.

I had an office in Buckingham Palace and commuted daily from Guildford, having moved a little further up the line from Haslemere. My job was to look after all the travel arrangements for HRH, land, sea and air; to accompany him on visits when required and to deal with some of the routine correspondence. All flying arrangements were made through the Captain of The Queen's Flight at Benson, whether using Queen's Flight, other RAF or commercial aircraft.

The Captain of The Queen's Flight was Air Vice-Marshal Sir Edward (Mouse) Fielden, whom I soon realized was a very remarkable man. He had founded the King's Flight as a flight lieutenant in 1936 when it just consisted of Edward VIII's personal aircraft, his DH Rapide G-ADDD. By now The Queen's Flight consisted of three De Havilland Herons, one of which was for Prince Philip's personal use, two Westland Whirlwind helicopters and a De Havilland Dove. The Dove had been allocated to the Flight in 1953 for HRH's flying instruction and was subsequently used for all his official flights until the Flight was re-equipped with Herons. Mouse Fielden stood no nonsense – if he met a problem he couldn't sort out himself he would pitch in at the highest possible level. It was from him that I first heard the expression when he said one day, 'John, never mess about with the monkeys, go straight to the organ grinder.'

He set extremely high engineering standards that resulted in exceptional reliability. For instance, all critical mechanical components were changed at half their usual life and he would not accept, for example, the normal limits for magneto drops on piston engines, or even the permitted level of leakage from air or hydraulic reservoirs. Nor would he accept 'red line entries' on the Forms 700 – these are faults which do not affect flight safety and which would normally have been accepted by the RAF. Consequently it took some time to bring a new aircraft up to his standards, but once it got there it tended to stay serviceable. This was well illustrated to me when I accompanied the CO of the Flight, Wing Commander Hyland-Smith, on a proving flight in one of the Herons to India and Pakistan in 1958 prior to the Duke of Edinburgh's visit the following year. We flew 120 hours in 29 sorties over 22 days, arriving home within 15 seconds of the scheduled 'doors open' time; there was only one minor unserviceability during the tour which was quickly sorted out. I had never experienced this degree of perfection in any aircraft I had previously flown in and was to enjoy these standards many years later when I myself became Captain of The Queen's Flight.

In January 1959 I accompanied the Duke of Edinburgh on his second world tour. He had previously undertaken a similar tour in 1957 when he visited the Antarctic, but this tour was to begin with a month in India and Pakistan, followed by sailing to the Far East in the Royal Yacht. We chartered a Comet Mk 4 from BOAC, with Peter Cane as the Captain, for the first part of the tour to India and Pakistan. Prince Philip did much of the flying from the right-hand seat and I quickly became impressed with his flying ability. Over the years I was to fly many times with the Duke and saw what a professional approach he had to aviation. He had already gained his RAF wings having been taught by my old friend Caryl Gordon, and since then had taken the opportunity to fly a number of different types. Whilst in India and Pakistan most of the internal flying was carried out in The Queen's Flight Heron. HRH invariably took the left-hand seat for the take-off and landing, but during the routine transits he would often return to his seat in the back to relax, have a meal, or more usually, to work on his speeches. Because he would always have been seen off by VIPs he did not want to keep them waiting whilst all the pre-flight checks were carried out, so these would have been done by the aircraft captain. Thus, when Prince Philip arrived he went straight to the first pilot's seat and everything was ready for him to start the engines immediately. When flying with The Queen's Flight he was always under the captaincy of a QFI and there was a perfectly clear understanding about who made the ultimate decisions – regardless of rank. I was to learn later that HRH always developed an excellent relationship with the aircrew with whom he regularly flew.

In India we had two interesting internal flights. The first was with an Indian Air Force Ilyushin IL14 to Agra and back to see the Taj Mahal. The IL14 was roughly equivalent to our Andover and this was my first flight in a Russian aircraft; to my disappointment it was uneventful. We were fortunate enough to see the Taj by moonlight; there was a low mist from the nearby river Jumna and this beautiful building appeared to be floating on that mist. It was a magical experience. The Taj, built in the seventeenth century, is so well proportioned that at 420 ft high it does not appear anything like as big as it really is. The other flight was from Delhi to Karachi for the second half of the tour of the subcontinent. This was in a Dakota of Indian Airlines and I was not particularly impressed when, during the take-off run, the Indian stewardess knelt down in the gangway to pray.

On a day when I was not required I went up to the Afghanistan border through the Khyber Pass. All the tribesmen seemed to be armed and we could hear the odd rifle shot from the nearby mountains where no doubt old scores were being settled. I doubt even now if we have learned the lessons of history in that remote and wild country.

From Pakistan we flew by Comet to Rangoon where we joined the Royal Yacht *Britannia*. The yacht was moored in the harbour and we sailed out to her in the royal barge. The relief of joining that wonderful ship after an intensive month in India and Pakistan, with continuous press intrusion and no chance for the Duke of Edinburgh to be able to relax or have a free day, was enormous. It was easy to understand why the Queen and Prince Philip, and of course all the other members of the Royal Family, had such affection for *Britannia*. From Rangoon we sailed to Singapore, Sarawak and Hong Kong where we were escorted to the quayside by a huge flotilla of local boats. It was a dramatic and picturesque scene. That evening I met some of the press in the hotel where I was staying and I remember the *Daily Mirror* man coming up to me and saying that, until that day, he had been a republican, but after seeing the Royal Yacht's dramatic arrival he had changed his mind.

We then sailed across the Pacific via the Solomon Islands, Gilbert and Ellice Islands and Christmas Island before going through the Panama Canal en route to the Bahamas and Bermuda. In one of the small Solomon Islands a Land Rover had been imported from a neighbouring island as a police car. It had 'Police' painted on the side and one of the islanders was asked to paint the same on the other side, so he painted 'Ecilop'. It was there that I heard pidgin English for the first time when Prince Philip was referred to as 'Him belong Mrs Queen'.

I was amazed at the standard of living and the wealth exhibited on some of the islands of the Bahamas where it seemed that every third house on the shore had a float plane moored alongside. At Exuma I met a retired squadron leader who was ADC to the Governor. He owned his own Cessna 180 float plane so, of course, I persuaded him to take me up. This was the first time I had ever flown off water and a most enjoyable experience it was. The weather was perfect during our visit; the sea was warm and a deep blue or that wonderful tropical green colour.

I have often been asked where I would like to live if money was no object and, despite all the problems created by our idiot politicians, I always say 'England'. I have had the good fortune to visit many wonderful locations around the world, but to me most of these exotic places seem to present two problems. First, I would want to live where I could be accepted as being 100 per cent part of the community, but even if one was fluent in the local language that would be unlikely to happen away from one's own country. Secondly, I have not been all that impressed with some of the expat Brits I met in these places. Many of them seemed to have gone there to avoid taxes, or to have cheap booze at the local golf club, or perhaps both. It just did not seem to be my scene.

From Bermuda we flew home in a BOAC Britannia. After three months away from the family it was good to get back. It had been a fascinating experience and the first time I had ever been to sea, apart from the odd local paddle steamer trip – what a way to start. As a former working member of the Royal Household on board *Britannia* I am permitted to wear the Royal Yacht tie which is something I often do with great pride. I was so brown when we arrived at Heathrow that I was mistaken by someone as the Pakistani High Commissioner.

Because I was involved with the planning of the Duke of Edinburgh's helicopter flights, I thought I ought to know something about these aircraft. I had already had the good fortune to be introduced to helicopter flying when I flew with Alan Marsh in the Sikorsky R4 way back in 1946. From that first flight I have always been enthusiastic about helicopters because, not only were they fun – and quite difficult – to fly, but I saw the enormous potential for their future use. However, it was early days and there was little point in my changing direction at that time because the fixed-wing career path still offered far more scope.

After I returned from the World Tour I saw the opportunity of doing a short helicopter 'Staff Officers' Familiarisation Course', at the Central Flying School at South Cerney, flying the Sikorsky S51 Dragonfly. This was an excellent course giving a short introduction to rotary wing flying to those staff officers who might be involved with the planning of helicopter operations. We practised all the likely situations such as engine–off landings, flying into confined spaces, landing on slopes, and so on, and we were also sent solo – another type. I am proud of the fact that I learnt to fly helicopters before automatic computerized gadgets were introduced to make them much easier to fly. One of the reasons I enjoyed helicopter flying so much was that they were a bit of a challenge, not just when taking off or landing, but all the time. It was said that 'a helicopter is an assembly of 40,000 loose pieces flying more or less in formation'. Many years later I heard Sir George Edwards talking about the designing of Concorde; when asked whether he had ever been involved with helicopters, he replied that he had not because he had spent all his energy trying to make sure that the wings on his aircraft stayed still.

At that time – the 1950s and 1960s – RAF pilots were expected to keep in flying practice when they were doing a ground tour. Aircraft were established at White Waltham for this purpose and I managed to fly fairly regularly in their Chipmunks, Ansons or Doves. This was obviously a most enjoyable commitment, but several years of occasional flying in a Chipmunk did not mean you were in flying practice on operational types like, say, Meteors. Perhaps this is the reason why we lost far too many senior officers in the early days of jet fighters. The policy was subsequently changed so that, if you were posted back to operational flying, you were given a refresher course on a jet aircraft followed by the full course at the Operational Conversion Unit for the type you were due to fly. I was to benefit from this policy on two subsequent occasions. However, since pilots were no longer expected to keep in flying practice during their ground jobs, I presume that is why we lost the establishment of those light aircraft.

Although I had achieved my ambition to fly in the King's Cup Air Race I was keen to do it again. I had no spare cash so somehow I had to try and do it for free, or at least at minimum cost. Perhaps I could find a rich owner who wanted a jockey. I consulted the Secretary-General of the Royal Aero Club, Colonel 'Mossy' Preston, to see if he had any ideas. He immediately said I must join the Tiger Club and he then put me in touch with the Founder and President, Norman Jones. According to Lewis Benjamin's book *The Tiger Club, Volume 1*, Norman had founded the Club the previous year in 1957 at Croydon and Fairoaks with the aim of providing Tiger Moth pilots with opportunities for competitive sport with light aircraft, whether it be racing, aerobatics, displays, rallies or touring. It had been formed by an experienced band of racing pilots whose aim was to help the ordinary club pilot to gain the necessary experience to enjoy first-class sport at as little cost to him or herself as possible. The Club does not undertake ab initio training and membership is not automatic, acceptance being judged on the merits of the applicant. According to the Members Handbook a member of the Club undertakes, inter alia (a) 'always go out of his way to assist other members in aeronautical matters', (b) 'always to fly with courtesy and with special attention to the safety of others', and (c) 'never to use an aeroplane for a disreputable or unworthy purpose'. The flying was certainly cheap at 30s (£1.50) per hour. This all seemed pretty good to me and I was promptly accepted as a member.

Norman was also Managing Director of Rollason Aircraft and Engines Ltd at Croydon and he was building the Rollason Turbulent under licence from the

Pilots of the Tiger Club were reminded that 'All Aeroplanes Bite Fools.' Photographed in the cockpit of Turbulent G–APNZ.

French firm Druine. There were several Turbulents in the Tiger Club and Norman invited me to meet him at Fair Oaks to fly one of these little aircraft. I was enchanted. The Turbulent, which sold at that time for only £950, is an ultra–light aircraft with a wing span of 21 ft and weighing only 345 lbs when empty. It is powered by a modified Volkswagen car engine. It was designed for the home–builder and is a delight to fly, but has to be treated with respect because it is not exactly over–powered. Perhaps that was why Norman put a plaque in the cockpit of each Turbulent: 'ALL AEROPLANES BITE FOOLS'. I had two flights in a Turbulent before we went on the World Tour, and after we returned I took every opportunity I had to fly with the Club which was then operating out of Redhill. I became a member of the Club's Turbulent team and took part in many of their displays.

I hoped to be able to enter the National Air Races in 1959 flying a Turbulent. Norman thought it would give a tremendous boost to the light aircraft movement in general if the Duke of Edinburgh would agree to enter a Turbulent in the races, with me as the pilot. This HRH very kindly agreed to do. Norman then set about preparing a new aircraft for the races that year. The aircraft was to be painted in HRH's colours, white with a green flash, and with his badge painted on the side. The Royal Aero Club agreed to let me have my old racing number again, No. 7. Norman built the aircraft to go as fast as possible and one of the modifications was to cut the windscreen down by several inches so that the slipstream only just passed over the top of my head. It took four men only

Flying Turbulent 'PNZ' over Ascot on its second flight in company with the Gemini of Flight Magazine. The Flight Collection

six weeks to complete. Norman carried out the first test flight of this aircraft, G-APNZ, from Croydon and I flew the second. The same day I took PNZ to Fair Oaks to team up with *Flight* magazine who wished to take an air-to-air shot of Prince Philip's entry from their Miles Messenger. The following day I was appalled to see our picture taking up the whole of the centre page of the *Daily Mirror*. What I had not realized whilst I was formating on the Messenger was that we had flown through a prohibited zone around Windsor whilst a race was being run below at Ascot. I expected to finish up in the Tower at least, but on reflection I think everyone was far too intent on the finish of the race – the horses can just be seen below the wing – and the shouting of the crowd would have drowned out the noise of our light aircraft above. Anyhow, no one made any complaints although these days I would no doubt have had a note from the Health and Safety Executive for not wearing a hard hat and ear defenders.

The National Air Races in 1959 were held at Coventry and the handicappers seemed to have judged our speed fairly accurately because we came 4th out of 14 in the first race, a class race, and 13th out of 18 for the King's Cup itself. However, we were 7th out of 42 in the British Air Racing Championship. We were the slowest aircraft and therefore first to take off in the King's Cup. Our speed overall was a mere 88 mph which is less than half the speed of a Formula 1 racing car. However, speed, like size, is not everything.

Negotiating one of the turning points during practice for the 1959 King's Cup Air Race. Photographed from Flight Magazine's Gemini. The Flight Collection

The day after the King's Cup I took part in the Club's Esso Tiger Trophy competition which was in the form of a so-called voltige. My French dictionary described a voltiger as 'someone who flutters or flies about'. This sounded fairly apt because the competition had to be flown in a Tiger Moth and within five minutes one had to take off, climb to 1,500 ft, do a loop followed by a second with a half roll on the way down leading into a slow roll and then a stall turn. With whatever height was left the sequence ended with an engine-off spot landing. This was good fun and I was very thrilled to win it that year.

One of my fellow cadets during flying training was Peter Latham who, by now, was commanding 111 Squadron, the Black Arrows. This was the squadron which, when led by Squadron Leader Roger Topp, looped a record 22 Hunters in formation at the SBAC Farnborough Air Display in 1958. I witnessed this phenomenal performance and, as far as I am aware, the record has never been beaten, or even repeated.

Peter and I thought it would be fun to produce a photograph of the Turbulent apparently leading the Black Arrows. This would have to be faked because there was a difference of some 75 knots between the maximum speed of the Turbulent and the minimum safe formation speed of the Hunters. We therefore took the photograph from another Hunter as the formation overtook the Turbulent. It caused a certain amount of amusement when it was published in *Flight* magazine. To quote from the copy of 9th October 1959:

> Closely 'escorted' by three Hunter F.6s of No. 111 Squadron – in an unfamiliar straight and level role – is the Turbulent G–APNZ which bears the Royal Arms and is flown by the Duke of Edinburgh's Equerry-in-waiting, S/L John Severne. What looks like a straight forward formation picture on the Service Aviation page this week was, in fact, an extremely sharp coup d'oeil by Air Ministry chief photographer 'Mick' Chase and the pilots concerned. As the Turbulent was doing about 85 mph flat out after a dive, and the Hunters were closing in at about 140 mph with flaps down, Chase (in a Hunter T.7) had to press the shutter at exactly the right microsecond. The result is a charmingly theatrical piece of deception.

In fact the Hunters were doing about 160 mph, but it's still a good story.

I persuaded Prince Philip, who by now was an honorary member of the Tiger Club, that he would enjoy the experience of flying an ultra–light aircraft with an open cockpit. I also thought the publicity would give a further boost to the light aircraft movement and sport aviation in general. He readily agreed and flew PNZ from White Waltham on 24th October 1959 becoming the first and, to date, the only member of the Royal Family to fly a single-seat aircraft. He enjoyed the flight, but complained that the top of his head got a bit chilly; I had forgotten that the windscreen had been cut down to my height to reduce drag, but since HRH was taller than me his head would therefore get caught by the

Turbulent 'PNZ' pretending to lead Peter Latham and Hunters of No. 111 Squadron. Photographed from a two-seat Hunter with Flight's photographer.

I swing the propeller of Turbulent 'PNZ' for Prince Philip while Norman Jones, the founder and chairman of the Tiger Club, looks on. The Flight Collection

Prince Philip lands 'PNZ' having become the first and only member of the Royal Family to fly a single-seat aircraft. The Flight Collection

slipstream. Twenty-nine years later I was reading Lewis Benjamin's book about the Tiger Club in which he wrote about Prince Philip's flight in the Turbulent. He said:

> What isn't generally known was that the little VW engine, which had been hotted up by Derringtons of Kingston for the races, failed on the next flight. It's idle to speculate all these years later, but at the time we fervently thanked the gods above that the engine didn't let HRH down, but instead put the wind up an unknown Tiger Club pilot, who glad to say got it down in one piece. There is a postscript which isn't without a gentle irony. John wound up as an air marshal and Captain of The Queen's Flight. I don't think we ever told John of his Boss's near miss; and it's a bit late now.

No they didn't.

Norman felt we could improve on our performance for the 1960 races and he set about making a number of improvements to PNZ. He put a sliding canopy over the cockpit, one which could be opened in flight; he fitted spats over the wheels; he installed a highly tuned, more powerful engine which increased the cubic capacity from 1192 to 1300 cc; fairings were fitted to all the struts to make them more streamlined and he installed a coarse pitch prop; but most significantly he fitted a Ford V8 twin choke carburettor which

Taken before flying in the King's Cup Air Race at Coventry in 1960. I came first flying No. 7 wearing my daughter's riding cap as a crash helmet, while Clive Francis came second in No. 2. The Flight Collection

considerably increased the power, and the fuel consumption. A second Turbulent, G-APZZ, was also modified, but not quite to the same degree and this was flown by Clive Francis. All this was, of course, declared to the handicappers, but they seemed to have misjudged the effect of the carburettor because we won the class race which was held at Cardiff and we were then favourites to win the King's Cup at Coventry. Norman, however, was worried that my engine might blow up and he put his money on Clive. When I received the starting time from the handicappers shortly before the race I knew that I ought to be able to win it; we even considered throttling back a little to protect the engine, but I decided to go flat out and we won by a handsome margin at a speed of 105.5 mph with Clive coming second in PZZ. I also won the British Air Racing Championship that year. *Flight* magazine, when writing about the race, finished up by saying: 'The question is: will John Severne be handicapped to win any race in a Turbulent ever again?'

The following year we entered the London to Cardiff race which started from Panshanger. *Flight* magazine had been right because we came 27th out of 40 starters despite achieving 107 mph. The King's Cup was due to take place that year at Coventry, but it was cancelled due to high winds.

During my time with HRH I accompanied him on many visits in the UK 'in attendance'. To me the most fascinating was a visit to the Isle of Wight to see the world's first practical hovercraft, Sir Christopher Cockerell's Saunders Roe SR-N1. We sailed/flew in this amazing machine and I realised we were travelling in something completely new when we sailed from the sea up a concrete slipway and there was no sensation of having transferred from sea to land.

In November 1961 I accompanied the Duke of Edinburgh when he and the Queen made an official visit to West Africa where I had the extraordinary experience of being in attendance on Prince Philip when he dined with President Nkrumah; no one else was present. It was soon after Ghana's independence and the President was a somewhat controversial character at that time. It doesn't take much imagination to realize that I witnessed a very unusual frank and fascinating discussion. There is a fine statue of the President in Accra with inscriptions on its base which go some way to explaining why, in the past, some countries have sought independence before they were ready for it. The two inscriptions read:

'SEEK YE FIRST THE POLITICAL KINGDOM AND ALL OTHER THINGS SHALL BE ADDED UNTO IT'
'WE PREFER SELF GOVERNMENT WITH DANGER TO SERVITUDE IN TRANQUILITY'

Thus ended a marvellous three and a half years working for Prince Philip. I was often asked if I minded being effectively out of the RAF for so long and I would then point out that I believed it was not only a rare privilege to be able to serve the Royal Family in a personal capacity, but I also felt I learnt far more about the armed forces in general, and also how the country was run, than if I had not had the job. In addition, I travelled to many places that I certainly would never have normally seen. I remain eternally grateful.

Shortly before I left in 1961 I had a private audience with the Queen who invested me with the Member of the Victorian Order (MVO). A few years later this decoration was renamed Lieutenant of the Victorian Order (LVO). To receive this award on a private occasion is a tremendous privilege, but it did mean that Katharine was denied the opportunity to enjoy the excitement of attending a public investiture.

Although I had been promoted to Wing Commander whilst I was still working for the Duke of Edinburgh I realized I was unlikely to progress any further without first attending a course at a staff college. Unfortunately there was a qualifying exam in the way which, for the previous six years or so, I had been trying to pass. The problem was that I kept on failing a different one of the three papers each time and unfortunately I had to retake them all again the following year rather than just the one I had failed. The Air Secretary's department wanted to send me to Staff College after my time as Equerry, but could not do so until I passed the dreaded exam. I had almost given up any hope of succeeding when I was called to the Ministry for a somewhat difficult interview and told: 'You are going to pass this time, aren't you.' So, with that encouragement, I swotted even harder than I had previously done, nobly aided by my wife who used to take our three children out for a picnic to leave me swotting in peace. I took the exam again, somehow managed to get through and was posted to the 1962 Course at the RAF Staff College, Bracknell. I probably hold a record by taking the exam five times before passing and finally getting on the course.

Chapter 9

A Passion Indulged

During my time serving that 'Unusual Appointment' I had the opportunity occasionally to indulge in my passion for flying light aircraft. My contacts in the Royal Aero Club and the Tiger Club led me to some very generous owners who were brave enough to let me fly their aeroplanes and most of the civil types listed in Appendix 2 were flown during this period.

Each type had its own story to tell, but perhaps one of the most intriguing one began in 1959 when Viv Bellamy, the Chief Flying Instructor at the Hampshire Aero Club at Eastleigh, invited me down to fly his Currie Wot. This little 22 ft wingspan, single-seat, ultra-light biplane had been designed by Joe Currie in 1937 for engineering students to build as an exercise. Whilst Joe Currie was building the first aircraft he got fed up with people asking what he was going to call it. 'Call it Wot you blooming well like,' he said and the name stuck. He built two aircraft which he offered at a price of £250, but unfortunately they were both destroyed during an air raid in 1940 at Lympne.

In 1958 Viv persuaded Joe Currie to let him use the original drawings to build a third Wot at Eastleigh. Like the first aircraft, it was fitted with a 36 hp JAP J-99 horizontally opposed twin cylinder engine. After a short briefing from Viv I flew this aircraft, but I can't say I particularly liked the engine which appeared to have the odd 'flat spot'. However, the overall impression was one of sheer elation as I climbed away from the airfield. I had been airborne for only a few minutes when I realized to my horror that I had failed to do up my straps – worse still, I must have forgotten to do the entire pre-take-off checks. There is no possible excuse for this, but my explanation at the time was that I must have been so overcome by the excitement of the occasion that I simply forgot. This dangerous omission was a salutary lesson and I certainly learnt about flying from that.

This third Wot was subsequently fitted with a 62 hp Czechoslovakian Walter Mikron engine and it then became known as the 'Hot Wot.' It was later fitted with floats to become the 'Wet Wot', but this version was not successful and the floats were soon removed. The original JAP engine was re-installed and the aircraft sold to Harald Penrose, the Chief Test Pilot of the Westland Aircraft Company. He christened the aircraft 'Airymouse' and wrote an enchanting book with the same title about the joys of flying this delightful little aircraft.

Viv Bellamy then built a fourth Wot with a Walter Mikron engine. This was subsequently fitted with a 60 hp Rover TP60/1 industrial gas-turbine engine, a similar engine to the one that powered the world's first gas-turbine-driven car. This aircraft was the world's first gas-turbine powered biplane. The story goes that he had a problem finding a suitable propeller because the first one he fitted had too coarse a pitch and taxying became somewhat interesting due to the high idling speed of the engine, and the fact that the Wot had no brakes. He told me that he was discussing this in the club bar when he noticed a propeller hanging on the wall and thought the fine pitch looked about right, so he took it down, found that it was out of balance, took a bit off the heavy end and – hey presto – it worked beautifully! He called this version the 'Wizz Wot.' I flew this remarkable aeroplane and am proud of the fact that I have flown the world's first single-engined turbo-prop biplane, and also the Balliol Mk 1 which was the world's first turbo-prop single-engined aircraft.

Around this time I flew to Thruxton one weekend with the Tiger Club Turbulent team and arranged to meet my old friend John Urmston who lived not far away. When I was at Cambridge on the 'RAF Short Course' he was in a nearby college studying medicine and we got up to all the usual pranks that undergraduates get up to. Later, when I was instructing at Cranwell, he had joined the RAF as a National Service medical officer and we had the pleasure on one occasion of flying together in a Prentice – the first time we had flown real aeroplanes together rather than models. Knowing that he was a talented model engineer who had built a 5in gauge engine and a railway track around his garden, and thinking that the Turbulent was really just a grown-up model aeroplane, I thought John might be interested in our little aircraft. In fact he was indeed so interested that he decided that very day to learn to fly and it was no surprise to me that he subsequently decided to build his own aircraft. He looked at several designs, but the plane had to be small enough to fit into his house whilst it was being built and the Wot, fitted with a Walter Mikron engine, seemed to him to be the ideal choice. His book, *Birds and Fools Fly*, is a most entertaining description of how he came to build his Wot and in my opinion is an absolute must for those contemplating building their own aircraft. Before John's Wot was finished he asked me if I would take it up for its first flight when the time came, but I declined to do so. I had every confidence in the aircraft because I knew it would have passed a number of very strict inspections from the Popular Flying Association at all stages of its construction, but I said there can be no greater personal achievement than to build an aeroplane and then to fly it yourself for the first time. He agreed to do that first flight and I was interested to read in his book: 'The person who stepped out of my

John Urmston with the Currie Wot he built himself. John Urmston

aeroplane after the first flight was in some way changed from the one who climbed in. A small flame of inner satisfaction had been kindled, a personal Everest climbed.' I subsequently flew John's Wot when he flew it up to RAF Coltishall for a Battle of Britain air display; but more of that later. I can therefore look back with much joy at my flights in the Wot, the Wizz Wot and now the Hot Wot.

By 1969 John Urmston had restored a 1931 vintage Puss Moth to flying condition and this he flew up to Elstree – we were living at the time at Stanmore – to present me with a copy of *Birds and Fools Fly*, the foreword to which I had written. In signing his book for me he wrote: 'To John Severne

John Urmston (right) with the DH Puss Moth he restored.

who was, not a little, responsible for all this. Delivered by Puss Moth, 29th March 1969.' He then kindly let me fly his Puss Moth with him sitting in the back and I was struck by the fact that its handling and performance compared very favourably with modern, mostly American, light aircraft, which made me wonder what had happened to progress in the intervening thirty or forty years.

The Tiger Club owned the one and only Arrow Active which I flew once from Fairoaks. Only two were built – Alex Henshaw baled out of the first one, the Mk 1, after it caught fire in the air, and the second one, the Mk 2, was rebuilt for Norman Jones and the Tiger Club. This strongly built metal single-seat biplane, with a wingspan of 24 ft, had been built in 1932 and it was certainly an exciting aircraft to fly, mainly because it had a fearsome reputation for being difficult to land and even to take off – as evidenced by the number of times it had been crashed. Alex Henshaw, in his book *The Flight of the Mew Gull*, wrote: 'I think I made that machine do everything it was possible for a biplane to do. I practised all the normal manoeuvres like loops, rolls, upward rolls and spins constantly, but it was such things as flick rolls, inverted spins, inverted gliding and tail slides and 'bunts' that I found more difficult and realised they had to be treated with respect.' The Arrow certainly looked good

The exciting Arrow Active flown by Martin Barraclough and photographed by John Blake. John Blake

and I remember enjoying looping, rolling and inverting the Active, so much so that I subsequently fantasized with planning a display routine, but never got around to putting it into practice. Lewis Benjamin wrote in his book *The Tiger Club – a Tribute*: 'Of all the Club's aircraft this must surely be the most exciting and not a little frightening.' It was fine in the air, but it lacked directional stability on the ground and would ground loop if you let it. Luckily it behaved itself when I flew it, and I still look back on that day as one of my many aeronautical highlights.

The Tipsy Nipper was similar to the Turbulent although it had a tricycle undercarriage and the advantage that it was fully aerobatic, which meant it was a lot of fun. However, it had a closed cockpit and it was not possible to open the hood once airborne which, to me, was a huge disadvantage because one of the great pleasures of flying Tiger Moths, Turbulents and other open-cockpit light aircraft is the exhilaration of having one's head in the fresh air. Being able to open the hood in flight gives one the best of both worlds.

The Comper Swift was a well known pre-war racing aircraft and I was fortunate enough to be allowed to fly G-ABUS from Sywell. This splendid little machine had a Pobjoy engine and was as exciting to fly as it looked. When a Comper Swift with a Gipsy III engine was entered by the Prince of Wales in the 1932 King's Cup Air Race, Flight Lieutenant Fielden, HRH's personal pilot, flew the aircraft in to 2nd place at a speed of 155.75 mph. This makes an interesting comparison to my speed of 105.5 mph when I won the race in the Tiger Club's Turbulent for the Duke of Edinburgh twenty-eight years later. Progress?

Flight Lieutenant 'Mouse' Fielden lands the Comper Swift which he flew in the 1932 King's Cup Air Race. The Queen's Flight Association

One day I was taken out for lunch only a few miles from Kidlington. We flew from the airfield in a Piper Super Cub 150 and landed minutes later in a field alongside a pub – a striking example of the use of a light aircraft. The Cub is not aerobatic, but it has a very impressive short field performance and it occurred to me at that time that a light aircraft can be run for little more than the cost of running a medium-sized family car; the snag is that you also need the car.

Looking back on this period many years later I realize how lucky I have been to be able to spend so much time in the air experiencing the sheer joy of flying a wide variety of light aircraft.

Chapter 10

The Lightning

By the time I managed to pass the Staff College qualifying exam I was getting a bit long in the tooth and was, by then, a wing commander. Consequently, after leaving that 'Unusual Appointment', I arrived at the RAF Staff College at Bracknell at the beginning of 1962 and found myself as the senior student. I learnt a great deal from the course and in many ways it made up for the fact that I did not have a degree. We were expected to type our solutions to the various exercises and I had therefore previously taught myself to touch type using a Pitman DIY book. This was in the days before personal computers and I bought myself a very nice small portable typewriter on which to practise. After six months or so I could touch type at about 30 words per minute; this really paid off because I found I was able to complete my exercises as much as half a day earlier than some of my fellow students who were still struggling with their one-finger typing.

I think the most important lesson I learnt on the course was the need to be able to prioritize one's work when under pressure. The directing staff would issue us with several exercises at the same time, some to be completed by yesterday, some by next week and some by next month. When under pressure the tendency was to forget the long-distance exercises and to concentrate on the immediate ones, but of course, the long-distance problem would eventually catch up with you if you were not careful and you would then find yourself working through the night to get the job done. Many of the exercises were joint exercises with the Royal Navy and the Army staff colleges and these were very good value.

One of my chores as senior student was to arrange for an end-of-course production of some kind to be put on by the students for the benefit of the staff. Luckily we had amongst us a talented scriptwriter, some good singers and an excellent producer. I myself did not take part because I am no good at that sort of thing, but the show was entitled – not by me – 'All this and Severne too!' It was a great success.

* * *

I managed to pass the staff course, but certainly not with any distinction, although this did not prevent me from landing the best job at the end of the course that I could have possibly hoped for. I was to go to RAF Middleton St George in Co. Durham (now Durham Tees Valley Airport) as the Officer Commanding Flying Wing. The wing consisted of two flying units: the Fighter Command Instrument Training School flying the Javelin, and the Lightning Training Squadron. The Javelin had been in service since 1956, but the Lightning, our first supersonic fighter, was newer, having entered service with 74 Squadron in 1960. The Lightning was a huge step forward from the Hunter and Javelin era and I greatly looked forward to getting to grips with this magnificent aircraft.

But first, since I had not been flying operational aircraft for five years, I needed to do the one month course at the School of Refresher Flying at RAF Strubby in Lincolnshire. We flew Meteor Mk 7s, the dual-control training version, and Mk 8s, the single-seat fighter version. The Mk 8 had an ejection seat whilst the Mk 7 did not. Looking back, I think I was fortunate not to run into trouble during my time instructing on the Mk 7 at CFS because it would have been difficult to bale out of an aircraft at high speed if it did not have an ejection seat. It was, however, very good to get back to some serious flying, but it took me a little time to regain my old form.

We had already moved into our married quarter at Middleton St George on 30th December 1962 in the middle of a very harsh winter, when the snow was just right for building an igloo that we could actually get into in front of our house. One has to wonder how often this will be possible in the future with so much talk about global warming.

I had never flown a Javelin, so the first thing I needed to do after I had completed the refresher course was to do the Javelin Conversion Course consisting of some twenty-five hours flying in the Mk 3 dual-control version. The Javelin was our first delta-shaped fighter. It was a fine aircraft, but it needed to be treated with great respect because of the very high drag created if 'the angle of attack' – the angle between the attitude of the aircraft and the direction in which it is flying – was allowed to become too high. Problems could arise, in particular, if you allowed the speed to get too low on the approach to landing, a problem aviators call 'getting on the wrong side of the drag curve'. Also, if the angle of attack was allowed to get too high the tailplane and elevators could become shielded from the clean airflow and that could cause all sorts of nasty problems.

When Duncan Sandys in his 1957 White Paper stated that manned military aircraft would soon be a thing of the past, the government cancelled almost every advanced aircraft project in development, but luckily the Lightning was too far along the road. In 1954 the prototype English Electric P1 had flown supersonic in level flight on only its third sortie, and this without re-heat. It was the first British aircraft to exceed Mach 1 (the speed of sound) in level flight and was soon to exceed Mach 2. The Lightning soon became one of my favourite aircraft – it was a delight to fly because, despite its stunning performance, it had few vices and most pilots had little problem in converting from lower performance aircraft such as the Hunter and Gnat despite the higher workload.

However, it was a different story for the ground crews – the aircraft was much more complex than any of its predecessors and it took some time for the engineers to get on top of it. It is the only twin-engined fighter to have one engine on top of the other, and the very narrow fuselage left little room for the engineers to get at some of the problem areas that arose.

The 60-degree swept wing was likely to result in a Lightning cartwheeling on landing if the pilot attempted to land with one wheel stuck up. We were therefore told to eject rather than attempt such a landing, a policy that was proved correct when an undercarriage leg collapsed on landing at another air-field shortly before I arrived. Although the aircraft was dramatically wrecked, it was astonishing that both pilots survived unhurt.

The Lightning was designed for the cold war era at a time when 'massive retaliation' using nuclear weapons was the preferred strategy of deterrence. If any defence was possible under these circumstances, it centred on being able to knock down Soviet bombers before they could launch their weapons, some of which were of the stand-off variety. The Lightning was therefore optimised for rapid climb to height, acceleration to supersonic speed and then to destroy

One of the undercarriage legs of this Lightning collapsed on landing at Wattisham. Miraculously neither of the two pilots were injured.

the bombers using air-to-air missiles in time to allow our Nuclear forces, predominantly the Victors and Vulcans, to get airborne. This was deterrence in action; if the Soviets believed that our nuclear forces could not be taken by surprise, then they would think twice about attacking us. The aircraft designers obviously got it right because the time taken from releasing the brakes at the beginning of the take-off run to reaching the cruising altitude of 36,000 ft (nearly 7 miles up) was exactly 1½ minutes. This was very exciting flying.

But things were changing. Mutual Assured Destruction (MAD!) looked increasingly futile, and a period of 'flexible response' was emerging. This was a recognition that a credible conventional defence backed by a range of nuclear weapons offered a more realistic strategy. Consequently the Lightning was required to intercept at long range as far as the Iceland Faroes gap, and to deploy as far as the Middle East. And this it did very effectively using Air-to-Air Refuelling, firstly with the Valiant and after that aircraft's demise, the Victor. Later this was augmented by fitting the aircaft with a bigger ventral tank and over-wing tanks for deployment. It speaks well for the design that the Lightning seemed able to adapt to these changed requirements with few problems.

The Lightning Conversion Squadron was commanded by Squadron Leader Ken Goodwin, himself a very experienced display pilot. He founded the 'Ten Ton Club', membership being confined to those who had flown 1,000 mph in a Lightning. Needless to say there was a tremendous demand to be taken up in our two-seat aircraft to qualify for membership.

When I was learning to fly the Lightning I found it more difficult to land than any previous aircraft I had flown. I think the fact that it was a heavy aircraft which landed at about 150 kts (about 170 mph) meant that judging when to begin 'rounding out' was critical. It took me about twenty hours before I could more or less guarantee making a good landing, whereas I had achieved this much earlier in any previous aircraft I had flown. Incidentally, we were told in the ground school that the energy required to stop a Lightning on the runway was the equivalent of lifting an elephant up 500 ft and then cooking it! It was also a difficult aircraft to operate, as opposed to just flying it. Previous all-weather fighters, from the Mosquito through to the Javelin, had a navigator to operate the radar and to navigate, but the Lightning pilot had to do the navigator's job as well as his own. On the right-hand side of the instrument panel in the single seat aircraft, was the radar screen which provided a host of information and included roll indications. The radar itself was operated by a hand controller which was equipped with a daunting number of switches and buttons on the left next to the throttles. Operating the radar with the left hand while flying the aircraft with the right hand could result in a very high work load. Naturally, we Lightning pilots like to think that only the best people were selected to fly this magnificent machine. It is an interesting fact, however, that a

The arrival of No. 226 Operational Conversion Unit at Coltishall from Middleton St George. The joy of flying is surely etched on our faces. From L to R: John Curry, Kit Thorman, JS, Jim Jewell, Les Harrison. Eastern Daily Press

remarkable number of very senior RAF appointments in the coming years seemed to have been held by ex-Lightning pilots.

The Squadron was equipped with the two-seat, dual-controlled Mk 4, but six months after I arrived the squadron expanded to become No. 226 Operational Conversion Unit and my appointment became Chief Instructor, which also encompassed the responsibilities of OC Flying Wing. Shortly after that we received additional Mk 1 single-seat versions. The OCU aircraft had a dramatic colour scheme which had been designed by one of the instructors – the spine on top of the fuselage was red leading to a red flash on the leading edge of the fin. Also on the fin was painted the badge of our reserve wartime squadron, No. 145, depicting a sword and shield, and we called ourselves the Crusaders. Training units flying operational aircraft have a wartime role, hence a reserve squadron number, in the same way that most servicemen in non-operational jobs have 'war appointments' which they immediately take up on the outbreak of hostilities.

With Middleton St George being one of the stations that ran a Battle of Britain display each year, as OC Flying Wing I was responsible for organizing the display and for its supervision on the day. One of our Lightning instructors,

Al Turley, who was a member of the Tiger Club, displayed the Turbulent I used to fly. Part of his display was to fly under a string with flags on it which was supported by two 10 ft poles held by a couple of stalwarts. Al and his wife Dawn were owners of a Proctor and Al has never been allowed to forget that his wife only took seven hours to fly solo, whilst Al took nine.

We had a serious problem at Middleton St George with a large roost of starlings, in a wood just off the edge of the airfield, which was nearly in line with the runway. Birds can be bad news if you hit them, especially at high speed – a big one can do serious damage to the airframe. The engines can usually ingest a few small birds without too much damage, but a large number of them going into the engine at the same time can put the bonfire out. When the starlings returned from their daily excursions, they flew in huge streams, some as long as half a mile, right through the approach path at about 150 ft. If a Lightning had flown through this stream it could well have suffered serious engine failure and could have crashed. We therefore had to stop flying for the half hour period when the birds were due home.

The strange thing was that the starlings' departure procedure from the roost was quite different from their evening arrival. In the evening they flew home in dense streams from different directions, according to where they had been feeding. In the morning they departed in a series of expanding concentric circles, like the ripples from a pebble thrown into a pond – we could see this clearly on the Air Traffic Control radar. The departure of the birds was not a problem because they were not concentrated together.

There are various conventional methods of persuading birds not to use airfields, but none of those methods seemed to prevent our evening flow of starlings. So we took advice from an ornithologist who said we would have to remove the roost – but how? He said that it was no use making a lot of noise once the birds had settled; they would just duck down and go to sleep. Similarly we had no way of diverting the stream once it was on its way. The trick was to create one hell of a racket just as the birds were about to land, which they did not like. We were told that it would probably take about a week before it had any effect, but it was worth trying. If nothing had happened after a week, they were probably never going to leave.

We organized teams of volunteers armed with such high-tech equipment as hammers and dustbin lids, Very pistols, thunderflashes, whistles, and so on. We positioned vehicles with radios trying to spot the direction of the flow – the driver would then radio to the team by the wood so that they could rush round to meet the birds as they approached, waiting until they were about to land before creating our cacophony. Just imagine a bunch of grown men rushing around banging dustbin lids and letting off thunderflashes – it was great fun and much enjoyed by those of us taking part. However, all our efforts had no effect whatsoever for about a week and then, just as we had been told, one evening they never returned. Indeed they never came back at all. Success at last. We were able to see on the radar where they had gone. They had chosen a wood about 10 miles away – but we never let on to the new landlord where his 2m starlings had come from. We now have starlings in our garden at home, and to make up for my anti-social behaviour over forty years ago, they are well fed and made very welcome.

I should have realized that RAF Middleton St George was due to close because a new Electronics Centre had recently been built there – it was quite remarkable how many stations closed soon after the completion of major building projects. Thus on 13th April 1964 I led a formation of 226 OCU aircraft from Middleton St George to RAF Coltishall in Norfolk. This was the famous Battle of Britain airfield where Douglas Bader had developed his 'big wing' tactics. I was determined to arrive overhead at Coltishall, in close formation, exactly on time. Having planned to fly one of the single seat Mk 1s, I previously flew the exact sortie in the simulator to help me with the navigation. This was a great help and I was pleased that, on the day, we were only 15 seconds late.

The following day I flew with our Station Commander, Group Captain Roger Topp, in a Mk 4 Lightning. I was amazed at how well he flew the aircraft bearing in mind that he had not flown for six months or so whilst Coltishall's runway was being resurfaced in preparation for our arrival. In retrospect I should not have been surprised because he was the same Roger Topp who had looped those twenty-two Hunters; furthermore he had been a test pilot at Boscombe Down helping to develop the Lightning.

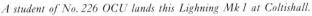

A student of No. 226 OCU lands this Lightning Mk 1 at Coltishall.

We moved into our new married quarter a fortnight or so before we flew down to Coltishall, my family consisting not only of my four ladies and our Black Labrador, Mr Jackson, but also our pony, Mourne, which we had acquired whilst we were up north. We had built a stable in our garden for her at Middleton St George and the journey down to Coltishall with the pony was one I shall never forget.

We had arranged to travel by train and British Rail had organized it incredibly well, with our own horse box and a compartment for a groom – me – so that I could look after Mourne during the journey. But first we had to get to the railway station at Darlington which was only a few miles from the airfield, so I rode the pony. The problem was that there was a very dense fog on the morning we left and I was seriously concerned that someone might run into us, but luckily they didn't. We had to change trains at Peterborough, but British Rail arranged for the horsebox to be shunted from one train to the other so that the pony and I were not inconvenienced in the slightest. Every so often the guard would come along to see if we were all right and I often wonder whether any of today's private rail companies would be able to provide such an excellent service. We had previously arranged to move Mourne into the old saddle club at Horsham St Faith, a recently closed RAF station just outside Norwich and only 10 miles or so from Coltishall. The saddle club was in a converted barn on the old airfield so I was even able to cut some hay for ourselves on our doorstep.

Group Captain Roger Topp lands Ken Wallis's autogyro at Coltishall. This aircraft was subsequently modified to become 'Little Nellie'.

In 1965 Wing Commander Ken Wallis, a friend of Roger Topp, flew one of his tiny single-seat autogyros to Coltishall for Roger and me to fly. Although I was by now qualified to fly a helicopter, I had never flown an autogyro. The difference between the two is that the rotor of a helicopter is powered directly by the engine, but the rotor of an autogyro is freewheeling and driven by the airflow while the conventional propeller drives the aircraft along. The handling characteristics of the two types are, however, totally different. The helicopter flies like, well, a helicopter, but the autogyro handles in much the same way as a fixed-wing aircraft – if you can fly a Tiger Moth you could fly an autogyro, but you would certainly not be able to fly a helicopter. It was a fascinating experience to become airborne after a run of only a few feet, perched on a seat and little else! Ken Wallis is a very clever aeronautical engineer and a perfectionist who was always developing his aircraft to improve them as he did not want to market them until he was completely satisfied. I suspect that the high degree of excellence he sought is virtually unobtainable, which is perhaps why his aircraft were never put into mass production. Nevertheless they hold all 20 of the UK official World Records for speed, time to climb, altitude, range and endurance for this class of autogyro.

This same aircraft, G-ARZB, was later modified with a smart cockpit nacelle to protect the pilot from the elements. Ken then flew it in the James Bond film *You Only Live Twice*, complete with missiles! Not many have flown 'ZB'. He

Ken Wallis flew 'Little Nellie' for the James Bond film You Only Live Twice. Ken Wallis

Wallis type WA-116 (XR-943) Autogyro 'Little Nellie'

told me recently that I am in good company because, among others, this delightful aircraft has been flown by Val Doonican, Gloria Honeyford and Genral Adolf Galland.

The Lightning course was divided into two phases, the first being the handling phase where the student pilot learnt how to handle the Lightning. The second was the more difficult phase where he learnt in addition how to operate the radar and the weapons system. Most of the instructors were ex-Lightning squadron pilots and were experts as operators. I never achieved their level of proficiency, but I used to carry out all the final handling checks at the end of the first phase of the course.

Soon after our arrival at Coltishall it was decided that we would take first-tour students. These were students who, after receiving their wings flying Gnats at RAF Valley, were given 60 hours flying Hunters at the Tactical Weapons Unit at RAF Chivenor before coming on to our Lightning OCU before joining an operational squadron on their first tour. Until then we had only accepted second tourists who were already experienced operational pilots, mostly from Hunter squadrons. There was much sucking of teeth from the old hands, but I remembered that I had been in much the same position when I started on the Mosquito, with no prior operational or twin-engine experience, and I had coped. Furthermore, I believed the young pilots would still be used to learning and I had no qualms at all about the new policy. The first four students were those who had been the best pilots at the Hunter OCU. I well remember flying with one of them on his final handling test because, to my delight and astonishment, he gave me a better ride than I had ever had from one of the instructors. The new policy was thus fully justified.

In 1964 I persuaded John Urmston to bring his Wot to Coltishall for the Battle of Britain air display and needless to say took the opportunity to fly his plane, the first time I had done so. It was good to fly the Hot Wot after the original Wot and the Wizz Wot – John had certainly done a marvellous job in building this delightful little machine.

My last day with the OCU at Coltishall was on 1st June 1965, the day of the Air Officer Commanding's annual inspection. The AOC was Air Commodore Al Deere, a famous New Zealand Battle of Britain pilot. My last flight was to lead twenty Lightnings in a fly-past for the AOC. Such fly-pasts usually consist of all available aircraft flying by in close formation, but I wanted this one to be different. We decided to take off at ten-second intervals – in re-heat thus making as much noise as possible – the first aircraft returning overhead at high speed, still at ten-second intervals, just as the last aircraft left the ground. I would finally land the leading aircraft just as the last of the high-speed aircraft flew overhead. The idea was that, for ten minutes, there would be a non-stop

John Urmston flew his Currie Wot to Coltishall for the 1964 Battle of Britain Air Display.

stream of aircraft either taking off, flying by at high speed or landing – in the event I have to admit that by then the ten-second interval had become a bit ragged. Anyhow, it was a wonderful way to bow out and I still look upon my Lightning days as amongst the very best in an interesting, exciting and thoroughly enjoyable flying career.

The Lightning stayed in service until 15th April 1988 when I attended a guest night in the Officers' Mess at Binbrook entitled 'The Last of the Lightnings'. It was attended by a very distinguished gathering including the Chief of the Air Staff, Marshal of the Royal Air Force Sir Keith Williamson (himself a Lightning pilot whom I had taught to fly when he was a Cranwell cadet), Roland Beamont who first flew the prototype in 1954 and many of the squadron commanders. The Lightning had been in service for 28 years, not bad for an aircraft originally expected to stay for only 10. It may have been light on fuel, but it was immensely powerful and manoeuvrable and it was certainly a joy to fly. It was the first and only all-British supersonic fighter to enter service with the RAF.

Chapter 11
Aden

After leaving Coltishall I was sent on the Joint Services Staff College (JSSC) course at Latimer in Buckinghamshire for the last half of 1965. I was pleased to be selected for the course, but I was a bit surprised because I had never seen myself as being in any way academically minded. It was, however, a very interesting and informative six months enjoying the company of students from all three services.

On our arrival we were issued with name tags. The directing staff encouraged us to use first names from Day 1, presumably to aid in the breaking down of any possible psychological barriers that might be thought to exist between the services. The use of first names was not, at that time, so universal as it is today. The Army and RAF students seemed to have no problem with this, but those in the Royal Navy appeared to have some reservations which we soon sorted out in the bar.

On the whole I think most serving officers are naturally joint service minded – certainly I had never experienced any problem at an operating level either with the Army when I was in Germany, or with the Royal Navy when I was subsequently at Kinloss. It seemed to us early on in the course that the problems began when senior officers were doing battle in London with the politicians and the treasury, and were pressing for the best deal they could get for their own service. When I returned to the JSSC on the directing staff after my next tour in Aden I remember well our introductory lecture at the beginning of the course. A very senior officer referred to the inter-service rivalry in high places and the first question asked by one of the students at the end of the lecture was, 'Sir, how senior do you have to be before you become un-joint?' Touché.

We did not own our own house until I was due to retire from the RAF, and since there were no married quarters available at Latimer we applied for a vacant quarter on another station. We were fortunate enough to be allocated

Positioning 'PNZ' for the static exhibition at the 1965 Battle of Britain Air Display at Coltishall.

one at Horsham St Faith which was very convenient because our pony, Mourne, was already stabled there on the airfield and the move from Coltishall a few miles up the road was a simple one.

In September Coltishall staged its usual Battle of Britain air display and I arranged for John Urmston to fly up in his Wot for the static display. I had asked my successor if I could display the Turbulent and so John and I left Redhill bound for Coltishall shortly before the weekend, with me setting off in PNZ ahead of John in his Wot who followed close behind. As we passed the Thames Estuary the weather deteriorated badly and John, very sensibly, decided to turn back to Redhill. We had no radio in those days and it was several minutes before I realized I was on my own.

After landing the Turbulent at Horsham St Faith I wheeled it down the road and parked it on the small lawn in front of our quarter, much to the amusement of some of the residents. John came up by train the following day and stayed with us. After the display I felt a bit groggy and John diagnosed probable appendicitis – the next day I had the darned thing removed. Luckily John was able to fly the Turbulent back to its home at Redhill on my behalf.

*   *   *

Shortly before the end of the course we received our postings and I was not too pleased to be told that I was to be sent to Aden. My concern was that I didn't think I would be able to cope with the heat, and I also thought it would be a very restricted life for the family because, due to the security situation, the families were not allowed up-country. It took me forty-eight hours to pluck up enough courage to tell Kath where we were going, whereupon she properly put me in my place by telling me that it would be one of our best tours to date. As usual, she was right.

Aden lies about 100 miles east of the southern end of the Red Sea. In 1839 the British East India Company landed Royal Marines there to stop attacks by pirates against British shipping en route to India. Aden then became an important station for the replenishment of coal and water, the port lying roughly equidistant from the important British possessions of Zanzibar, Bombay and the Suez Canal which opened in 1869. Aden was ruled as part of British India until 1837 when it became the Colony of Aden, a British Crown Colony. A large oil refinery was built by BP at Little Aden in 1953. After the closure of the Canal in 1956 Aden became the main military base for the British in the Middle East, the hinterland being loosely tied to Britain as the Aden Protectorate.

In order to stabilize Aden and the surrounding Protectorate from the designs of North Yemen, the British attempted gradually to unite the disparate states in the region in preparation for eventual independence. In 1963 the colony

The Federation of South Arabia before independence.

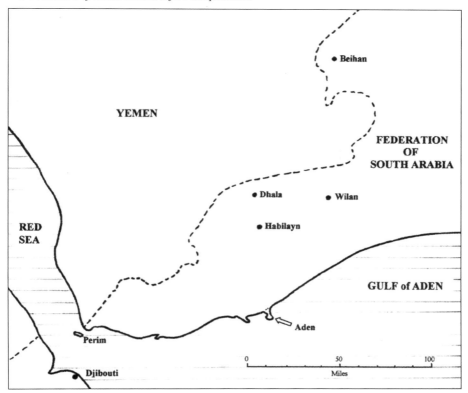

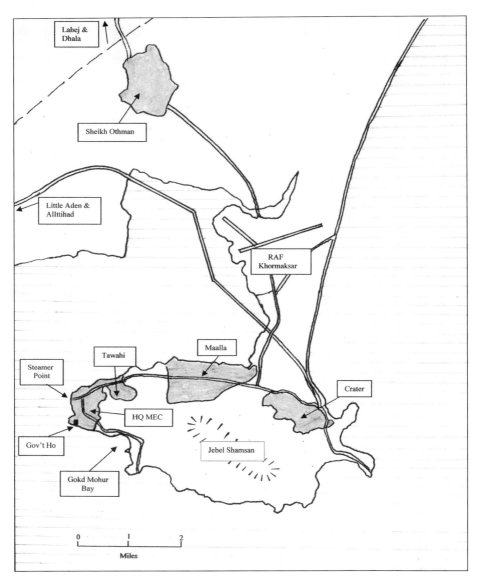

Aden State.

became the State of Aden and the Federation was renamed the Federation of South Arabia (FSA). The Federation would remain under British rule but was given a degree of autonomy with authority to establish its own armed forces.

An insurgency against British rule then began with a grenade attack by the National Liberation Front (NLF) against the British High Commissioner, killing one person and injuring fifty. A state of emergency was then declared. The following year Britain announced its intention to grant independence to the FSA in 1968, but the British military would remain in Aden. When I was at the RAF Staff College in 1962 a Foreign Office lecturer had told us that we would be in Aden 'for at least another twenty years'. He was wrong.

I went ahead to Aden on my own at the beginning of 1966 because it would be six months before a married quarter was likely to become available. Meanwhile, the family were allowed to remain in our comfortable quarter at Horsham St Faith. My job was to be 'Ops 2' in Headquarters Middle East Command which was a unified command with well-integrated staffs of the three services working very closely together. The Command covered a huge area from Kuwait to Botswana and Uganda to Madagascar. I could see that my time on the Joint Services Staff College course was going to prove to be invaluable.

My job specification rather grandly said that I was to be 'responsible for the policy and operation of the Fighter, Maritime Reconnaissance and Helicopter Force in the Command'. This involved working closely with the Army in order to provide day-to-day support from the helicopters provided by No. 78 Squadron flying the Wessex; the ground-attack aircraft from Nos 8 and 43 Squadrons flying the Hunter Mk 9; Photographic Reconnaissance from No. 1417 Flight operating the Hunter Mk 10 and maritime reconnaissance

The 'Ops 2' desk at Headquarters Middle East Command. We used to look forward to our leave!

The AOC lands the Wessex at Habilayn after re-supplying the troops in the field.

from the Shackletons of 37 Squadron. I also looked after the RAF Marine Branch unit and the Search and Rescue Whirlwind helicopter flight at Khormaksar which provided the Air Sea Rescue cover. The Hunters were, of course, fully converted for ground attack with four 20 mm cannon and the ability to carry sixteen 3 in Rocket Projectiles (RPs). They provided air defence, close support for the Army and also flew in the more traditional air policing role which included house demolitions, firepower demonstrations and 'flag waves' upcountry. The latter were sometimes effective by simply providing a presence overhead. One specialist form of this was to disrupt the dissidents' rest patterns by planting sonic booms on the target areas to provide the illusion of operations at night. The RPs were Second World War weapons which were difficult to deliver accurately because they had a slow velocity with a consequent large gravity drop. They also required very accurate flying by the pilot for about four seconds before releasing the weapon, not an easy requirement in the turbulent conditions often found in the mountains.

The Shackletons were used in the theatre to provide a capability for maritime patrol and for search and rescue. Their most extensive operational use at that time was during the Rhodesian oil embargo after Ian Smith had declared UDI, when the Shackletons were deployed to Majunga in Madagascar. From there they searched for and identified tankers bound for Beira in Mozambique, which would then be intercepted by ships of the Royal Navy – an operation that became known as the Beira Patrol. A good example of how aviators and aviation minded people can stick together was when the Shackletons had the occasional communication problem, only to find that their messages were being relayed by the Air Traffic Controllers at Salisbury (now Harare) – the 'enemy!'

The long endurance of the Shackleton gave it a good capability for providing top cover overland for troops or convoys moving through areas where there was an internal security threat. It could provide effective suppressive firepower using the nose turret's twin 20 mm cannon, and also by dropping bombs of various weights. In the press releases of the day these were euphemistically referred to as 'aerial grenades'.

Flying in the Arabian peninsular at that time was serious aviation. During 1966 and 1967 no less than twenty-three aircraft were destroyed or damaged by hostile action in the air or on the ground, including a Hunter which caught fire in the air after being hit by a rifle bullet, and a Dakota of Aden Airways which was shot down.

When the family came out we were allocated a flat literally on Tarshyne beach at Steamer Point. It was delightful. The children were at boarding schools at home and flew out for the holidays, unaccompanied, on specially chartered aircraft which became known as the Lollipop Specials. The young seemed to enjoy the adventure and were very well looked after in the air and at the airports by the air hostesses.

The sea and swimming pools were always warm so the children spent most of the time in the water and consequently became very proficient swimmers. Sharks were a danger and our beach was therefore protected by a shark net. This was very necessary because, a few years earlier, an officer had been killed by a shark while he was bathing in shallow water.

One of my greatest relaxations was to go snorkelling to watch the wonderfully coloured fish. On one occasion I disturbed a small octopus and nearly got an eyeful of ink; I was amazed how quickly it could move if it wanted to. The shark nets were not foolproof, as I realized when I found a hole in the net whilst snorkelling. We therefore taught the children to make sure there were always other swimmers further away from the shore than they were – hopefully the sharks would get them first.

There were two distinct seasons. The summer was hot with a constant maximum temperature of about 104°F; the snag was that it was also very humid. Luckily we had air conditioning in our bedrooms and offices. The winters were like the best of an English summer with much lower humidity and the temperature a steady 82°. During each of the two seasons there was very little variation in the weather and it was always, or nearly always, sunny. In between the two seasons there were the monsoons. These lasted for about a month when there were occasional unpleasant sandstorms and the weather couldn't make up its mind what to do. Most of us found the summer climate difficult to cope with when we first went out, but after two weeks or so the body became acclimatized and I personally enjoyed it, despite my original forebodings.

There was one major exception to the concept of wall-to-wall sunshine. In April 1967, during our second year, we woke up one early morning with water dripping through the ceiling onto our bed. Kath said, 'It's raining.' I said, 'Don't be silly, it never rains in Aden.' But it *was* gently raining, in fact. By the time we went to work at 8.00 am it was raining hard. By 10.00 am a number of us were on the balcony of our Headquarters watching the torrents rushing down the road and going straight through the Communications Centre. At this stage the Commander-in-Chief, Admiral Sir Michael Le Fanu, joined us and simply said, 'I think this is serious.' In fact we had 6 inches of rain in seven hours. For a period we lost all communication with UK and I think they thought we had all been blown up. There is a 1,800 ft volcanic ridge, Jebel Shamsan, which overlooks Aden, and the water was rushing down the sides of the mountain, damaging the foundations of many of the blocks of flats in Maalla and washing away parts of the road between the HQ and the airfield at Khormaksar. Since 'it never rained' there were no storm water drains. By the afternoon the parade ground was flooded with sufficient water for people to be able to paddle their own canoes.

Each year we were entitled to two weeks leave in Kenya as part of our leave entitlement. This R & R (Rest & Recreation) period was important because most of us, especially the families, were living in a fairly stressful situation. Being able to look forward to a fortnight's relaxation away from it all in Kenya was a great morale booster. There was an excellent NAAFI-run leave centre, Silver Sands, on the beach near Mombasa and we had booked ourselves in there, together with our three young daughters, on the day of the flood. Somehow we needed to get the family out to the airfield at Khormaksar where a Comet of East African Airways was due to fly us out to Nairobi. The first problem was to get to Khormaksar. The road had been seriously damaged in places and it would have been a difficult journey by car, but I managed to persuade someone to take us there in a Land Rover which just about coped with the exciting journey. The second problem was that Khormaksar had lost communication with Nairobi and was unable to talk to the Comet, but the captain, who was well aware that he had a load of passengers desperate for a well earned break from the hazards of Aden, took it upon himself to come anyway. When we saw the aircraft land we could hardly believe our eyes and we shall always be profoundly grateful to that splendid airline pilot. We were told that the next day the slopes of Shamsan, normally sandy coloured, were green. Seeds which had lain dormant for years had come to life.

Our holiday was one of the best family holidays we have ever had. We spent most of the time at Silver Sands where at breakfast we were always entertained by the monkeys coming in and stealing bananas from our tables. We got much amusement from watching the fury of the African staff trying to deter them, but the monkeys always won. Whilst at Silver Sands we took a short three-day break to the National Park at Tsavo to introduce the girls to the excitement of a safari – nearly thirty years later they still talk about it.

The previous year Kath and I had taken our two weeks leave during term time, and had planned a holiday through a travel agent in Aden to tour Kenya in a car starting from Nairobi. This turned out to be a memorable trip, the highlights being our visits to Tree Tops, Lakes Nakuru and Naivasha, and also Kericho where there was a very comfortable hotel, the Tea Hotel. From there we had planned to drive the 100 miles or so to Keekorok, a new lodge in the Masai Mara Reserve, close to the border with Tanzania. When the hotel manager heard of our intention he said we were mad because the rains were due and we would most likely get stuck in the mud miles from anywhere. He then asked, 'Why don't you charter a light aircraft and fly there and back while we look after your car?' I said something about not being able to afford it, but when we looked at the cost, it turned out to be little more than what we would have had to pay for the mileage on the car and the petrol. At this stage I had some rather uncharitable thoughts about the travel agent who had recommended the itinerary. A few hours later a smart Cessna 210 arrived to take us to Keekorok. As our Turkish pilot landed on the short strip at the lodge an angry Ostrich ran alongside under the wing, its body language saying very clearly, 'Get off my b****y strip.' It was a very amusing arrival.

On our second day we went out in a Land Rover with an armed driver on our first safari – a magical experience for us to see so many animals in the wild.

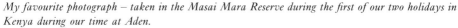

My favourite photograph – taken in the Masai Mara Reserve during the first of our two holidays in Kenya during our time at Aden.

Looking back, it was extraordinary that we were out all day and did not see another vehicle or human being – a far cry from today when one does one's best to avoid all the other zebra-painted minibuses.

While at Keekorok we learnt how a German zoologist, Dr Grzimek, and his son Michael had flown out from Germany in a light aircraft to carry out research in the Serengeti in general and in the Tanzanian Ngorongoro crater in particular. They were the first people to chart exactly where the huge migrations of wildebeest went each year. Sadly, Michael was killed when he flew into a vulture on the rim of the crater. We were so impressed with Grzimek's book, *The Serengeti Shall Not Die*, that we vowed to return one day to explore the crater.

The perfect way to enjoy the serenety of the bush.

It was to be another thirty-four years before we were able to keep that promise to ourselves. On that occasion we had the privilege of flying across the Serengeti in a balloon. It was a big balloon with fifteen or so passengers and we took off at dawn as we watched the sun rising. Ten minutes later our American pilot radioed to the ground party to say exactly where he wanted the breakfast table to be set up. Fifty minutes after that we landed 100 yards from a beautifully set table and enjoyed a marvellous breakfast, complete with champagne in black bottles labelled 'Cordon Negro', and all being served by formally dressed local staff. The pilot had been navigating to the site by changing height to find the right winds so that he could land as close to the table as possible. We had been flying with a second balloon and the two pilots had been competing with each other to see who could land the closest. We won.

During the flight we were sometimes so low that we could hear the long grass brushing against the bottom of the basket. We were so awestruck by the serenity of the occasion that we remained silent most of the flight; when we did speak it was only very softly. The respect that all the passengers paid was so impressive that I commented on it to our pilot afterwards. He just said, 'That's because you were a bunch of Brits. If you'd been Americans it would have been quite different.'

Back in Aden, with 1966 seeing a massive increase in terrorism, it was a difficult time with the NLF and the Front for the Liberation of South Yemen (FLOSY) trying to push us out of the Federation and the Crown Colony of Aden itself. The Arabs had never been particularly fond of us and once we said we were going anyway, there was little reason for them to remain loyal, either to us or the Federal rulers whom they were always being told were our stooges and puppet successors. This was driven home by a carefully planned programme of assassinations, and any Arabs who showed loyalty to Britain tended to be bumped off and left with a label tied to their necks saying 'the fate of all traitors'. They naturally concentrated on the local intelligence staff, police and special branch. There were thirty-six such assassinations in 1964 and no less than 1,250 in 1967. There had also been a number of nasty murders of British personnel and a few small bombs, mostly hand grenades thrown around. The huge car bombs of today, thank goodness, had not come on the scene at that time. We all had to take reasonable precautions such as searching our quarters and our cars daily, never going downtown alone and never advertising parties by displaying invitation cards in our homes. The military areas were well protected, but that did not stop a bomb exploding in the Officers' Mess at Steamer Point, the home of the Headquarters. Our local staffs were mostly Arabs or Somalis who had worked for the British for years. They were excellent people whose loyalty was not normally questioned, but we knew they could be put under intolerable pressure from the terrorists who might threaten their families if they didn't do the terrorists' bidding. Our own bearer, Said, was a Yemeni and a delightful fellow. He had worked for the British for many years and found it difficult to believe that we really were going to leave. Even when he finally accepted that we would be leaving Aden he said he would continue to work for the British. After I explained that the nearest British presence would be in the Gulf he said that was no problem, he would walk there with his family and his goats. He could not get his head round the fact that he would have to walk 1,500 miles or so across the desert.

In May 1967 strikes closed the harbour to commercial shipping and the situation was compounded when in June the Arab–Israeli War resulted in the closure of the Suez Canal. Although the Arabs were badly defeated by the Israelis our locals managed to put the blame on Britain, so the slogan of the day became 'a bullet against the British is a bullet against Israel' – which increased the resentment against us.

The Army was busy controlling dissident tribesmen upcountry and providing us with security at the base. A typical task might be for me to arrange for helicopters to position urgently needed army support, or for the Hunters to carry out a rocket attack to destroy a known terrorist's home. On one occasion I flew in a two-seat Hunter to witness the squadron carry out a rocket attack with eight aircraft targeting two houses and two arms caches belonging to a well known dissident leader in a village near Wilan. The cockpit temperature was closer to that of the centre of the earth than to that of the sky we were flying in, but it was very exciting flying. On landing my pilot, Squadron Leader Fred Trowern, said, 'And to think we get paid for this as well!'

On another occasion I had the privilege of flying in a Wessex of 78 Squadron when we positioned four soldiers in a remote unfriendly area to carry out a reconnaissance on some terrorists. I was astonished at the small size of the site which the pilot chose to land on because the helicopter blades were literally clipping the leaves of a tree. Three days later we picked up four very tired and dirty men; what they had been up to I have no idea, but I'm sure it was dangerous. That was the first time I had become directly aware of the sort of jobs these amazing men undertake.

Ground-attack pilots are often directed to their targets by Forward Air Controllers (FACs), who are Army or RAF officers operating from the ground or in the air. On one extraordinary occasion, I was a passenger in a Beverley which carried an Army FAC to direct Hunters onto three separate targets. I found it almost bizarre to be slowly flying over hostile territory, relatively low, in such a huge lumbering transport aircraft. In fact, it was quite safe because, unlike today, the terrorists did not have hand-held surface-to-air missiles; we only had to keep out of range of their rifles.

The Beverleys of 84 Squadron did a marvellous job when the local workers went on strike at the oil refinery at Little Aden. In order to keep the Hunters

A Hunter of No. 8 Squadron over Wilan.

The Hunters attacked two houses with arms caches belonging to a Well-known dissident in a village near Wilan.

Dissidents planted a mine at Habilayn which blew off an undercarriage leg of this Beverley. The driver of the Land Rover, Major Neville Read, was wounded by a grenade soon after I took this photograph.

flying the Beverleys ferried jet fuel in their own fuel tanks from Djibouti to Khormaksar. And talking of strikes, we witnessed a most amusing situation when the Aden bank workers went on a go-slow. We were drawing out some money from National Grindlays when we watched a bank clerk pushing a trolley full of files across the room. He was indeed going slow – literally. He gradually put one foot in front of the other, an inch at a time, and he must have moved fully six feet during the ten minutes that we were there.

I worked closely with the Army Air Corps and enjoyed several interesting flights in their Scout helicopters. Low flying with the Army is always quite an experience and one particularly exciting flight took us up the narrow mountain road to Dhala, in the north of the Federation and close to the Yemen border. There is a rough strip at Dhala where I had previously landed in a Twin Pioneer and had witnessed a novel way of starting a reluctant engine. The ground crew wound a rope round the spinner of the propeller – rather like starting a toy top – and attached the end of the rope to a Land Rover which then drove off. The engine had little option but to start, which was a good thing because Dhala would not have been a sensible place in which to be stranded. Back in 1964, Claire Hollingworth, a well known war correspondent, visited Dhala and subsequently wrote in the *Guardian* about an interview she had had with a tribesman from the Radfan. He said that the reason they attacked the road to Dhala was the fact that they hated roads because they hated wheeled vehicles. These were depriving the tribesmen of their trade in camels and all sorts of other things associated with travel by four-footed animals. But he went on to say that they considered aircraft to be all right because, after all, the Prophet travelled on a carpet (which I never have, so a carpet is not one of the types listed in Appendix 2). However, that didn't seem to stop them from shooting at every aircraft they saw.

I subsequently accompanied our AOC, Air Vice-Marshal Andrew Humphrey, to witness the first landing of a Hunter at Beihan to see if it was a safe strip for them to use. There had been several incursions by MiG-17s from the Yemen and the local ruler had asked for our protection. The MiGs were operated by Egyptian pilots flying from San'a, the capital of the Yemen, the aircraft and the finance also being provided by the Egyptians. The Hunter, piloted by the Officer Commanding the Strike Wing, Wing Commander Martin Chandler, landed and departed safely, but it was decided not to let the Hunters use the strip after all. It would have been too dangerous to leave the aircraft on the ground at Dhala, but if they were scrambled from Khormaksar, about 100 miles away, the MiGs would have departed long before the Hunters could have arrived. So there was not much we could do about it, much to the annoyance of the ruler.

The RAF has always run survival courses for aircrew likely to fly over water, arctic, jungle or desert terrain. Since I was responsible for the Desert Survival Course at Aden I thought I had better see what goes on. I therefore joined a course which began when one of our Air Sea Rescue launches dumped us on the remote island of Perim at the foot of the Red Sea. We had emergency rations and kit to distil water from the dew – not very much, but enough for survival. It was a relief to be picked up several days later and to be able to quench one's thirst. I learned several good lessons from that short course, one of which was that I had not realized how incredibly unpleasant it is to be really thirsty.

Not long after I arrived in Aden I was appointed Air Adviser to the South Arabian Government, the Federal Government set up by us at Al Ittihad, just outside Aden, to run the country after we left – at least that was the intention. I was told to form a South Arabian Air Force (SAAF), by independence, consisting of a balanced force of transport, communications, helicopters and ground-attack aircraft – all for £2m. Although I already had a heavy workload I had no staff to assist me in this extra commitment, presumably because this was deemed to be just a secondary duty.

The MOD contracted Airwork Services Ltd who had considerable experience in this field and they found the aircraft for us. The Crown Agents on behalf of the British Government bought four Dakotas with new engine life and fully refurbished for a mere £25,000 each. The Dakota, although an old aircraft, was ideal for rough up–country transport work. New and much smaller Skyvans were offered at £500,000 which we could not possibly afford. I wanted to buy six Alouette helicopters from France, but since all purchases had to be made in sterling we had to buy the only option available, the Westland-Bell 47 Sioux, despite its pathetic performance in hot conditions and at high altitude. Although our first choice for strike aircraft was the Strikemaster, none were

The first of four Jet Provost Mk 52s for the South Arabian Air Force.

available, so BAC refurbished and modified four ex-RAF Mk 4 Jet Provosts to
Mk 52 standard capable of carrying weapons. One of these aircraft, serial
No. 104, was sold to the Singapore Air Force in 1975 where it served until
1980. It is now owned and flown in its original SAAF colours by Swords
Aviation of North Weald. Finally six Canadian-built Beavers were purchased,
the Beaver being a rugged single-engine aircraft designed for bush operations. I
was responsible for approving the design of the aircraft markings and also the
uniforms. Wing Commander Barry Atkinson MBE DFC RAF was seconded
as the Commanding Officer and Airwork recruited the pilots and civilian
engineers.

Choosing the right weapons was a problem because the requirement was
to put a missile through the front door of a terrorist's house. The old 3-inch
Rocket Projectile still being used by the RAF was not exactly a precision
weapon and I therefore looked around for something better. The RAF at that
time was introducing rockets called SNEB, but they were too expensive a
weapon for us because, to be sure of hitting a small target, you had to release
the whole pod of 16 rockets in a ripple. Airwork then came up with the SURA
rocket, a remarkable weapon made by Hispano Suiza of Switzerland which
Boscombe Down tested for me. Boscombe confirmed that SURA was so
accurate that if there were any target errors, they were the pilot's. I subsequently
learnt that the neighbouring Sultan of Oman's Air Force (SOAF) was so
impressed with the weapon when they saw us using it that they also bought it –

so at least I suppose I did SOAF a good turn. This was a period when a number of cases of corruption concerning the sale of aircraft had been exposed, although I did not expect them to offer me a cash handout because I like to think that they knew it would not be accepted by a Brit. I was, however, delighted when Hispano Suiza offered me a small Swiss Army knife as a thank you for buying their weapon. A gift which, I hasten to add, I gladly accepted.

Britain gave South Arabia £5m for the running of their armed forces and by Independence all the aircraft except two of the Dakotas were in place, as were the eighteen pilots who were all British except for a Belgian, a German and a Czech. The engineers were British civilians and all were under contract to the South Arabian Government. Squadron Leader 'Rags' Barlow, an RAF navigator who had taken early retirement from the service, was appointed as the Operations/Intelligence Officer; he also acted as Adjutant to the CO.

Nearly forty years were to pass before I was able to find out what happened to the SAAF after independence. I was recently giving a lecture to the Taunton and Tiverton Branch of the Aircrew Association when one of the members attending the meeting happened to be 'Rags' Barlow and he was able to tell me about their unpleasant experience in the hands of their new masters.

On the granting of independence on 30th November 1967, the Federation of South Arabia was immediately renamed the People's Democratic Republic of Yemen (commonly known as South Yemen). The Air Force was renamed the People's Democratic Republic of Yemen Air Force (PDRYAF) and within days the old South Arabian markings were removed and replaced with the new markings of the Republic. At the end of February 1968 the South Yemen Defence Minister, after visiting Moscow to seek financial aid for their armed forces, gave a distinctly anti-British broadcast in which the South Yemen Air Force was accused of passing information concerning every move of the Government to the British Embassy. The British Government had previously instructed the South Yemen Government that the Air Force was not to operate outside its own border. British pilots were flying for Saudi Arabia and our government wanted to avoid the possibility of Brits fighting Brits. This was considered by the South Yemen Government as intolerable interference. On 27th February all the British personnel of the Air Force were ordered to assemble in their crew room for an address by the Minister of Defence. Speaking through an interpreter he said that the Air Force had been controlled by the British Embassy and not by himself. He therefore had no further use for their services. During the address the building, hangars and aircraft had been surrounded by Arabs with machine guns, some being pointed through the crew room window. The officers were promptly arrested. Two buses took them to the British Embassy, but they were later allowed to go to the Officers' Mess, under armed guards, to collect their belongings. Rags Barlow had the uncomfortable experience of having to open all the safes with a gun in his back.

Some of the families had arrived the month before and they were given one hour to pack and to be prepared to leave. The following night was spent in a compound at the airport before they were all flown back to the UK early the next day, their contracts terminated without compensation. Subsequent protracted discussions with the Foreign Office failed to result in reasonable compensation for the breaking of the contracts and the financial penalties suffered by our personnel. To this day they still feel they were badly let down by our government. Soon after the dismissal the first Russians arrived with some MiG-15s and they were subsequently to form the mainstay of the South Yemen Air Force.

While the Foreign Office had announced that we were to give the Federation independence in 1968, the date was being kept secret for security reasons. When George Brown finally announced to the House of Commons, some two weeks beforehand, that the date would 29th November 1967, the shooting stopped immediately, indicating that the terrorists were well controlled by NLF and FLOSY. This was just as well because plans had been made for us to make a fighting withdrawal if needs be.

The plan was for the heavy and bulky items to go by sea and that people, including the families, would go by air together with the smaller valuable items. Equipment not needed elsewhere was to be sold locally. Since Khormaksar had already suffered several terrorist attacks it was thought that it might be too dangerous to operate a large number of troop-carrying flights out of the airfield. If necessary we would therefore be evacuated by sea to Masirah Island and flown home from there, a withdrawal that would be executed by a task force of the Far East Fleet. Shortly before Withdrawal Day (W-Day) the impressive task force assembled. It included the aircraft carrier HMS *Eagle*, which would provide air defence after the Hunters left, the two commando carriers and the assault ship HMS *Fearless* from which the final withdrawal would be controlled and where I was allocated a position in its operations room. In the event, when the shooting stopped, we were able to carry out an orderly withdrawal by air from Khormaksar.

The first phase of the withdrawal, Operation Relative, took place about six months before independence when the families were sent home. This meant that, at the same time, all the associated support such as schools, hospital and so on could be closed together with most of the married quarters. Many families, particularly those who lived in the Ma'alla Straight, had been through a very harrowing time – one of the Khormaksar aircrew had a rocket fired through his bedroom window when his wife and small baby were in the room. It was therefore somewhat of a relief to us when the families left. I accompanied Kath on the military bus to the airfield, a journey of 5 or 6 miles. On the way, going through the built-up area of the Ma'alla Straight, we were stopped by an Army patrol when a young subaltern came on board and said, 'There is a little shooting going on so we will be held up for a few minutes, but don't worry everyone, we will look after you.' He had an air of confidence about him and we consequently felt very reassured. The flight home for the families was a bit tedious because it got held up in Teheran when the aircrew ran out of their crew duty time.

After the families had left there were several visits from well known entertainers who gave performances in the open-air theatre. Two of the concerts stick in my memory because of their starkly contrasting characteristics. One well known comedian gave a quite unnecessarily blue show which I personally found offensive, but this was followed a few weeks later by Harry Secombe. I was told that he asked what sort of programme he should give and that he was advised to 'play it straight'. He gave a stunning performance which included many operatic arias. The troops loved it – so did I – and it just goes to show that comedians don't need to get cheap laughs from blue jokes in order to please their audiences.

The High Commissioner, Sir Humphrey Trevelyan, left the day before independence and so did I, although I hasten to add that there was no connection. The final aircraft left on the last day with the few remaining personnel, the last two passengers to board being Air Commodore Freddie Sowrey (the Senior Air Staff Officer) and Brigadier Charles Dunbar (the Brigadier General Staff), with the airfield protected by a company of Royal Marines who left by sea.

The High Commissioner, Sir Humphrey Trevelyan, departs by Britannia 28th November 1967, the day before Independence.

The morale of the Aden base was extremely high during our time there. Conditions were not ideal with a difficult security situation to deal with and a tiresome climate, but there was a strong feeling of everyone being in the same boat and co-operation between the three services could not have been better. I think it was a typically British approach – it seems that we are at our best when under pressure. It was certainly a memorable experience for me and my family and we are grateful for it.

Thus ended 128 years of British rule on 29th November 1967, a very interesting chapter in our colonial history. For the very small part I played during that time I was awarded the OBE.

Chapter 12

Jack of All Trades

I may have been surprised to have been selected to go on the Joint Services Staff College course in the first place, but I was even more surprised to be sent back on the directing staff at Latimer after leaving Aden. Presumably 'They' thought my Aden experience would be useful. However, after only four months I was moved again to Headquarters Strike Command on promotion to the acting rank of group captain. The fact that I was to be promoted after such a short time at Latimer presumably did not mean that I had disgraced myself there. As we had moved into a married quarter at Latimer only seven weeks earlier, this was the shortest time by far that we had stayed in one place.

We now took over a very nice married quarter in the town of Stanmore, which was administered by the nearby RAF station. It was quite unlike a standard quarter, had a delightful small garden and was the sort of house we would have liked to have owned. It was around this time that we made the conscious decision not to buy a house, even though prices were beginning to shoot up. The reason was that the law at that time was heavily in favour of the tenant and a number of our friends who had bought houses and then let them when they were posted, subsequently found that they had bad tenants who had not looked after their homes properly and, in some cases, had refused to pay outstanding rents or even refused to leave when required to do so. We were not prepared to have all that hassle and instead we bought ourselves furniture when birthdays came along, so that when the time came for us to buy a property, we would at the least have all the essentials that we would need.

My job was to be 'Group Captain Organisation' on the Administrative staff of Headquarters Strike Command. The main HQ was actually at High Wycombe, but the administrative staffs were at Bentley Priory, Stanmore. This was a big commitment and I was really thrown in at the deep end with responsibility for building projects throughout the Command, for personnel establishments and for all those niggling administrative jobs that no-one else wants to take on.

Fortunately I had a very wise and helpful boss who guided me through the first difficult months and I also had a very competent staff, so all in all I learned a great deal and, much to my surprise, I found myself enjoying it.

Of course I missed the flying. At Aden, while I did not have a flying appointment, I was at least dealing with flying matters and occasionally got into the air, but this job was a very long way from aeroplanes. Nevertheless, as a group captain, my ambition was to command a flying station when I left Stanmore and I realized that this job would give me valuable experience. Some station commanders have come unstuck in the past because, despite the fact that they were experts in the operational field, they had had little administrative experience to fall back on. I will never forget that earlier incident when a young airman had referred to RAF officers as 'a lot of spivs'. This had highlighted a newly commissioned pilot's lack of experience in man management.

I learned a lot about organization, particularly when I became heavily involved with the disbandment in 1969 of Coastal Command and the consequent formation of No. 18 Group within Strike Command. I was also involved with a number of major building projects and got to know the mysterious workings of MPBW, the Ministry of Public Buildings and Works. I remember attending a meeting to decide how best to restore the main building at Bentley Priory, a famous listed building. I said I thought the first thing was to get some painters on the job to repaint some of the window frames to keep the damp out. 'You mean brush operatives,' said the chairman. I kid you not.

My staff were responsible for the planning of a new Air Staff building at HQ Strike Command, High Wycombe. We visited a number of recently finished projects before deciding on its style. One of these was the new headquarters for Training Command at Brampton. This was a lightly constructed building with removable internal walls so that the arrangement of offices could be changed without undue difficulty. One morning an officer coming to work found that his office door did not shut properly. Moments later others found the same problem. It seems that a helicopter had landed close to the building the evening before and its downdraft caused the whole structure to move slightly. Needless to say we did not adopt that style.

During my time the Officers' Mess at RAF Northwood, the home of Coastal Command, had been burned down. It was impressive to see that a new Mess appeared unusually quickly and I realised that it was possible for the whole planning and construction process to be sped up when a real emergency arose, but only at the cost of other priorities. During the fire many of the old Coastal Command files had been destroyed and some of us cynically thought how fortunate their staff were.

One afternoon, after I had been on the job for about eighteen months, I had a telephone call from the Air Officer Commanding-in-Chief, Air Marshal Sir Denis Spotswood, who said, 'I'm sending you up to Kinloss as station commander.' I replied, 'But sir, I've never flown a big aeroplane and I have never had anything to do with the maritime world.' Whereupon he said, 'That's exactly why I am sending you there and if you fly those things like Shackletons I will skin you alive!' The Shackletons had recently retired and had been replaced by the new Nimrod which was a huge technological advance over its predecessor.

Chapter 13

Hunting with Nimrod

Before taking up my appointment at Kinloss I needed to do a refresher course on Jet Provosts at RAF Manby because I had been away from serious flying for over five years. Then, I needed to learn about the new Nimrod and its maritime role by attending the full course at the Maritime Operational Conversion Unit at St Mawgan in Cornwall. During those three months at the end of 1970 we spent a happy time in our rented house overlooking the bay at Mawgan Porth which was only a few miles from the airfield.

In the air transport world pilots can spend several years as a co-pilot before becoming a captain – it must be very frustrating to fly hundreds of hours as a number two and not to be able to enter another type in the log book. I was therefore pleasantly surprised to find that in the maritime world we were sent 'solo' early on in the course with another student as co-pilot. It was only a short flight, but it was a tremendous morale booster to feel that you had actually flown this splendid new aircraft as the captain.

Since the late 1950s the Air Ministry had been debating the replacement of the piston-engined Avro Shackleton which was itself a development of the Avro Lincoln bomber which was a WW II design and had entered service in 1946. Indeed by the 1960s even the Mk 3 variant of the Shackleton was something of a relic thanks to its slow speed and dated sensor fit. Visual lookout was still a primary search aid although radar was reasonably effective at detecting surface vessels or submarine snorkels. However, the aircraft was unable to detect and track the nuclear submarines that were becoming more plentiful as the Soviet Navy was receiving enormous funding and was already a potent threat. It possessed a large and capable surface fleet equipped with state-of-the-art air defence and anti-surface vessel missiles, complemented by attack and ballistic missile-carrying nuclear-powered submarines. With much of the Soviet Navy located in the Barents and Black seas, and operating ever further afield in the Atlantic and Mediterranean, the Shackleton was ill equipped to cope, having fallen well behind the capabilities of other anti-submarine aircraft such as the

The Avro Shackleton Mk.3, the Nimrod's predecessor, showing the contra-rotating propellers. Military Aircraft Photographs

United States Navy (USN) P3 Orion – a development of the Lockheed Electra airliner – and the twin-engined Franco-German Atlantique. Already, Soviet submarines were operating off the West Coast of the UK with little chance of being detected.

A Ministry of Defence Operational Requirement called for an aircraft combining high transit speed and the ability to operate low and slow on patrol. By 1963 the in-service target date was set for 1968. A later requirement defined the tasks of the new aircraft as including anti-submarine warfare (ASW), surveillance of sea and land forces, area surveillance, the ability to carry out limited air-to-surface strikes against enemy vessels, search and rescue, and the ability to carry out emergency trooping.

The short timescale and comprehensive requirement suggested that a new design was not an option. Serious consideration was therefore given to both the French-designed Atlantique and the USN P3. More appealing to the politicians were proposed adaptations of the VC10, the Trident, the Vanguard and the BAC 111. The RAF preferred a four-engined all jet solution, and at this stage Air Chief Marshal Sir Harry Broadhurst, then Managing Director of Hawker Siddeley, decided to enter the fray with an adaptation of the

A Lockheed P3 Orion of the US Navy, a possible contender as a successor to the Shackleton. Military Aircraft Photographs

Comet 4C. Legend has it that the outline design was completed and submitted within three days. Certainly, by 1965 Hawker Siddeley were authorized to proceed with the development of the HS 801, and in January 1966 an order was placed for 38 aircraft. The first flight was in 1967, and the first aircraft was delivered to the Maritime Operational Conversion Unit in October 1969. It was a really wonderful achievement to develop, test and equip a new aircraft – albeit based on an old design – on time and remarkably quickly at a cost of £100 million for the entire batch.

The name for the HS 801 was debated for many a long week, but in 1967 the then AOC-in-C of Coastal Command, Air Marshal Sir Paul Holder, eventually sought help from the Bible and in the 'Book of Genesis' in Chapter 10 he discovered 'Nimrod, a Mighty Hunter before the Lord' and decided that this was an apt name.

Although the Nimrod was recognizable as a development of the Comet 4C, it was powered by four of the more powerful Rolls Royce Spey engines, each developing 12,160 lb of static thrust. It could transit at airline altitudes at 500 kts, operate 1,000 miles from its base, on task for up to six hours at low to medium altitudes, and then return home. Up to four short-range French AS12 air-to-surface missiles could be carried under the wings and other weapons were carried in a ventral pannier that ran for almost the entire length of the aircraft. Mk 44 Active Torpedoes were the main Anti-Submarine Warfare (ASW) weapons, but nuclear depth bombs (NDBs) could be carried for use against deep submarine targets. As you would imagine, the training of both air and ground crews for the carriage and handling of NDBs was extensive, but only representative 'shapes' were ever carried.

Active and passive sonobuoys could be carried and used to refine the position of an underwater target in order to mount an attack. Once dropped into the water, the sonobuoys float and a hydrophone – an underwater microphone – is deployed to a pre-set depth. The active buoys are only effective over short ranges and are used to refine the position of a submerged submarine target so that an attack can be mounted, by emitting an acoustic ping that is reflected from the underwater target back to the buoy for transmission to the aircraft. The passive sonobuoys are designed for the long-range detection and tracking of the very low frequencies transmitted through the water by vibrations created by submarine propulsion units. Fortunately, each type of propulsion unit, nuclear or conventional, emits a unique energy pattern and processing of the information in the aircraft can allow the crew to make a specific identification of a submarine type. Of course, ships too cause energy patterns and these emissions often travel very long distances making the local environment very noisy, often masking the frequencies of interest. At the time, one active sonobuoy cost the equivalent of a new Mini car and the allocation per crew for training was very limited, so most of the training was undertaken in the new simulator. Air Sea Rescue equipment could also be carried in the weapons pannier enabling dinghies and other equipment to be dropped to airmen who had landed in the sea, or to distressed seamen.

There is nothing secret about a sonobuoy itself, but on board the Nimrod the electronics which interpret the message sent by the sonobuoy are highly classified. I was told that shortly before I arrived at Kinloss a Nimrod crew had watched a Russian submarine surface and pick up one of our sonobuoys. They even heard the noise of the hydrophone clanking its way up the side of the submarine; then they heard voices in Russian, but had no idea what they were saying. All this was recorded and when they got home an interpreter translated one of the voices as simply saying, 'How do we switch this damn thing off?'

The ASV 21 radar was an updated version of the radar in the Shackleton and was positioned in a neat nose extension of the weapons pannier. But the greatest departure from the classic Comet shape was at the rear of the aircraft. The Electronic Support Measure (ESM) equipment, which could detect and identify unwelcome radar transmissions, was housed in a fairing on top of the dorsal fin, and a tail boom was introduced to house the Magnetic Anomaly Detector (MAD) as far from the metallic mass of the aircraft as possible. Great care had to be taken during take-off not to rotate too vigorously because it was easy to scrape the end of the boom on the runway. This equipment was to be used to refine a submarine contact so that an attack could be made. It could detect any magnetic anomaly to the earth's magnetic field caused by the presence of a submarine, but its very short range meant that, to be effective, the aircraft had to be flown in precise patterns only 200 ft from the sea surface – an interesting challenge. Finally, a searchlight was fitted in the starboard wing fuel pod for night-time identification of contacts, and again the aircraft had to be flown at very low level with the co-pilot operating the searchlight joy stick.

One of the advances in crew comfort was the inclusion of an electric grill which was used to cook steaks and hamburgers. Unfortunately the grill fume exhaust trunking passed into the conditioning system at a point close to a fire detector, and in the early days of Nimrod operation there were a number of spurious fire warning alarms that led to an emergency being declared as a result of the smoke created by a burnt steak. It took some months before the connection was made and the use of the grill banned.

When flying low over the sea through salt-laden air the engine and airframe are liable to suffer from corrosion, so after every such flight Nimrods are washed by a spray of fresh water. This is done automatically as the pilot slowly taxies the aircraft through the wash which is provided by an array of jets across the taxiway and which is quite dramatic when seen for the first time from the cockpit. The wash can be switched on by Air Traffic Control at the request of the pilot, which is obviously necessary – the mind boggles at the thought of a light open-cockpit aircraft suddenly and unexpectedly being doused in water.

Overall the aircraft was a major advance, and the much enhanced working environment was appreciated by crews brought up on the far more spartan Shackleton. The galley and toilet facilities approached airline standards. The cabin was quieter and the air conditioning was both comfortable and necessary to maintain a healthy working environment for the mass of new, but temperature-sensitive electronic equipment. In particular, some of the navigation equipment destined for the ill-fated TSR2 was transferred to the Nimrod, which explains why Nimrod was one of the first to have a partial inertial navigation system installed. This equipment was prone to overheat and

The Nimrod Fresh Water Wash. Tom Kidd Photograph. The Times, London, 1970

some adventurous navigators found that one solution was to transfer the equipment from the navigation crate to the galley cold box for an hour or so. Most importantly, however, the Nimrod provided UK fixed-wing crews with the ability to locate and track submerged submarines over considerable distances and with remarkable accuracy.

The decision to develop the Comet rather than the American Electra is open to question. The reasons for wanting to choose a British-built aircraft are obvious, but the P3 has some significant advantages over the Nimrod. There is more room in the rear cabin of the P3 for the crew and their sophisticated electronic equipment. There is also more space on the flight deck and the visibility for the pilots is better – the space enables a replica of the navigator's tactical display to be shown between the two pilot seats; in the Nimrod, such information has to be transmitted by voice over the intercom. The P3 is also faster at low level than the Nimrod although not as fast at high altitude; the Nimrod can therefore reach its operating area more quickly. The P3 can use a shorter runway and is easier to handle on ice. Perhaps the most significant advantage of the P3 is that the fuel consumption of its turbo-prop engines is less than that of the jet engines of the Nimrod and its overall operating costs are lower. It was unfortunate that the Nimrod came into service at the time of a fuel crisis in the early 1970s – its heavy fuel consumption was a significant factor in our inability to sell the aircraft to the Canadians, Australians, New Zealanders, the Indians and a variety of South American countries.

One advantage we currently have over the American aircraft is that the training of our crews appears to be of a higher order and we retain them in the role for longer periods. When electronic equipment fails, our operators are more innovative and seem to be able to go 'back to the chalk board'. This is significant operationally when the Nimrod crew might be able to continue operating, albeit in a limited fashion, after equipment failures, whereas P3 crews tend to pack up and go home. Interestingly, to back up this somewhat provocative statement, during the First Gulf War the United States Navy surface vessels preferred to operate with Nimrods in support rather than their own P3s.

I had just half a day with my predecessor before taking over and I still remember his final words: 'You will have a problem every day and a disaster every week.' What a cheerful thought. Sadly he was proved right. During my first week one of the Nimrod aircrew was killed one night driving home in the snow and shortly after that a small child, playing outside its own married quarter was run over and killed by a refuse lorry reversing. RAF stations are organized to cope well with such tragedies – apart from the obvious support from immediate family, friends and neighbours, most major stations have a resident padre and the administrative staff are trained to provide all possible help. Not least, the station commander's wife has a most important role to play in supporting the wives of all ranks, especially when their husbands are away on extended deployments. Our padre, who had only recently joined the RAF, soon appreciated the fact that he could call upon the administrative staff for help, a facility not normally available in a parish.

We moved into our new home at Kinloss in January 1971. The station commander's residence, Langcot House, was a delightful building on the edge of Findhorn Bay. It was a Victorian farmhouse and had been bought by the RAF just before the War, together with 48 acres of foreshore, for £2,500. But it had one small snag – it was very close to the end of the main runway. We did, however, have the luxury of double glazing on the sides of the house facing the airfield and this slightly reduced the noise. We managed to locate its last owner and invited her to tea. When I asked her whether she regretted selling such a lovely house for such a comparatively small sum, she just said, 'No, who on earth wants to live by the side of an airfield?'

Royal Air Force Kinloss.

It was a joy to live on the edge of the Findhorn Bay because there was so much bird life to watch. There were many varieties such as oyster catchers, all sorts of gulls, shelduck, plovers, curlew (with their delicious sounding cry), goldcrests (in our garden) and above all, the ospreys. The latter had recently been reintroduced to the area and there were several breeding pairs in the forest to the north of the bay. The locals were very good at protecting these birds and when visitors asked where the ospreys were, the locals would say, 'Ospreys, what ospreys?' The RSPB had erected a splendid hide at Loch Garten near one of the nests and visitors can see the birds and their young in their nests through powerful glasses a hundred yards or so away. This drew visitors away from the other nests which were consequently left in peace. One evening we had the privilege of watching an osprey teaching its young how to fish in the bay close to our house. The young were not very successful, but no doubt they eventually became operational. It is appropriate that the RAF Kinloss badge features an osprey.

The village kirk was also close to the airfield and because a Nimrod is very noisy when taking off we tried to avoid operating during Sunday services. However, there was one occasion when a Russian submarine had been reported off the coast of Northern Ireland and we were tasked to try and find it and to monitor its movements. Unfortunately this meant taking off during a service so I called on the minister at his manse afterwards to explain why we had broken our unwritten agreement. He smiled and just said, 'Och, it was nae bother, I just turned off my hearing aid!'

Kinloss is situated on the Moray Firth, east of Inverness, and is some four hours by road to Edinburgh and an expensive journey across the border to England. Most of us who were fortunate enough to have our families living with us greatly enjoyed the life, but it was a different matter for the single men and women whose friends and family were down south. I have been told that the present generation call the base 'Ice Station Kilo'.

Learning about the Nimrod and its fascinating maritime role was something quite new to me. Never before had I flown with a large crew – the most I had previously enjoyed was when I had just a navigator to keep me in order when flying Mosquitoes with No. 264 Squadron a quarter of a century earlier. The Nimrod, however, had a crew of twelve: two pilots and a flight engineer at the front end, and a whole team of clever people in the back who operated a variety of devices to look for and sink submarines. Previously I had flown fighters with a very short duration – the first Hunters I flew could only stay up for about forty-five minutes before they ran out of fuel – but the Nimrod could stay up for ten hours or so. I was therefore glad to find that there was a toilet and galley in the back.

We had two full mission Nimrod simulators at Kinloss which represented not just the flight decks, but also all the operational positions of the nine aircrew who operated the navigational, communications and weapons systems in the rear of the aircraft. Simulators have several valuable qualities. They help crews to keep in flying practice while at the same time being checked regularly for correct aircraft handling and, in particular, for their reaction to emergencies which could not be practised in the air, like engine fires. The cost per flying hour of a simulator is a fraction of that of the real aircraft so they are a valuable and economic training aid. They can also be used for developing operational tactics without spending expensive flying hours or taking any possible risks with real aircraft. Simulators normally have motion and sound which can represent to a high degree the physical and aural sensations experienced when flying, for example when turning or experiencing turbulence. They also have a visual representation projected on to screens outside the flight deck to show what the pilot would be seeing. Normal flying clothing is worn and it can all be made to feel so close to reality that many pilots have, on occasion, forgotten that they are still on the ground.

But as we all know computer-driven devices occasionally play tricks on us. I was starting my take-off run in a simulator one day when the 'aircraft' suddenly decided to take off like a helicopter and rise vertically, still in a horizontal attitude. According to the flight-deck instruments, and also the scene outside, we were rising very rapidly as the airfield disappeared beneath us. It was quite alarming, but also amusing. This is known as a 'glitch', an expression which I was told originated in America and stands for Goes Leary Intermittently and Then Completely Haywire – a very apt description of what most of us have experienced in some way with our own personal computers.

Like all the crews I used to carry out weekly simulator rides. I had a regular slot at 6.00 am on Monday mornings with my Wing Commander Operations, Mo Short, taking it in turns to act as captain and co-pilot. This enabled us to attend the 8.00 am briefing in the station operations room without disrupting our day.

It might be thought that flying a large aircraft would be rather dull after flying single-seat fighters, but let me assure the reader that flying low over the sea at 200 ft, at night, in bad weather, 1,000 miles out over the North Atlantic, concentrates the mind no end. Since jet engines are more efficient when running at high power, the fuel consumption when flying at slow speed when on patrol is less if three engines are running at high power, rather than four at low power. However, the aircraft must always be able to climb away after an engine failure, therefore before shutting an engine down, sufficient fuel must have been used up so that the aircraft is light enough to be able to climb away on two engines whilst the engine that had originally been shut down is relit. Towards the end of a mission, a Nimrod is even light enough, and the engines powerful enough, for the aircraft to be able to climb with only one engine running. Therefore, when the fuel state is low enough, the latter part of a patrol is conducted with two engines shut down. These procedures are practised in the simulator so that flight engineers know exactly what to do in order to relight an engine very quickly in the event of an engine failure. At least, that's the theory.

Losing an engine suddenly when operating on only two engines is obviously very alarming. On one occasion such concern became a full-blown 'Mayday' emergency. A Nimrod operating at around 12,000 ft at night over the North Atlantic on two engines suffered an engine failure and, despite all the simulator practice, the one remaining operating engine was shut down by mistake rather than the one that had failed. Fortunately, the altitude available allowed the crew to relight all the serviceable engines and a very shaken and chastened crew returned to Kinloss. The subsequent inquiry was assisted enormously by the engine and voice recorders (the black box) fitted to the Nimrod, and thus for the first time an RAF crew could be heard facing possible death in frightening detail with the expletives not deleted.

Intelligence would often provide an area of interest in which a Soviet nuclear submarine might be operating or transiting. For example, submarine transfers from the Northern Fleet to the Mediterranean via the Iceland/Faroes gap occurred quite often, and this offered them the opportunity to loiter off the approaches to Faslane and Holy Loch in an attempt to gather intelligence on UK and US submarine deployments. Similarly, any NATO maritime exercise in the Atlantic always attracted at least one Soviet submarine as an uninvited observer.

Occasionally we would find Soviet surface ships and these would be photographed for the benefit of our intelligence staffs. Before I arrived at Kinloss a Nimrod managed to photograph a Soviet Tu-16 Badger bomber circling one of their new helicopter carriers.

On one of my sorties we were specifically looking for a Soviet intelligence-gathering trawler in the North Sea. These ships were full of sophisticated listening devices and our intelligence staffs liked to know where they were. They looked like any other trawler in a fishing fleet except they were cluttered with aerials and were clean, whereas the fishing vessels were full of nets and whatever. This time the intelligence gatherer was in the middle of a huge fishing fleet of over 200 trawlers and we had to find the proverbial needle.

We were, of course, living at the height of the Cold War that I had previously experienced at close quarters as a fighter pilot in Germany. In this context the anti-submarine role is very interesting in that it is one of the few where the aircrews are doing almost exactly what they would be doing in wartime. Whereas bomber crews were obviously not able to practise flying to their assigned targets in the Soviet Union, and our fighter pilots could not practise attacking Soviet aircraft over their own territory, we on the other hand

A Soviet Tu-16 Badger circles over a Soviet helicopter carrier.

could operate over the same water that we would be flying over if hostilities should break out and we could search for and find real Soviet submarines. The only difference being that we did not sink them.

The maritime community across the Western world, and particularly within NATO, uses standard procedures so that ships, submarines and aircraft can operate together, regardless of nationality. This co-operation was first practised during the Battle of the Atlantic and has evolved as submarine and missile technologies have advanced. Needless to say, joint operations across nationalities had to be practised and honed. Soon after the War ended the Joint Anti-Submarine School (JASS) was established in Northern Ireland, but moved to RAF Turnhouse near Edinburgh in 1970 when its role was broadened to reflect the multi-role Cold War threat. The School was then renamed the Joint

Maritime Operational Training Staff (JMOTS) and ran several 15-day courses a year. Each course was attended by up to thirty British and NATO ships and submarines which assembled at the Clyde naval base. Supporting Anti-Submarine Warfare (ASW) aircraft from the UK and NATO forces operated from Kinloss, with other disciplines such as Airborne Early Warning (AEW) and maritime strike/attack using other bases. Thus Kinloss welcomed and supported these ASW aircraft, deployed for JMOTS, from most of the NATO nations. We always provided several of our own crews for each course. A few days of ground school was followed by work-up local exercises, and finally a major week-long convoy protection exercise in the deep waters off Scotland. Since my time at Kinloss, the ability for the allied nations to work successfully together in a hostile environment has proved itself time and time again from the Falklands to the Gulf and Afghanistan.

I flew regularly with all the crews from each of the three squadrons, Nos 120, 201 and 206, the crew captain taking the co-pilot's seat, allowing me to take the first pilot's seat. On only my second sortie in a Nimrod at Kinloss I carried out a liaison visit to the United States Navy at Keflavik in Iceland where they were operating the P3 Orion Maritime Patrol aircraft. We called it a 'liaison' visit, but it just so happened that it coincided with their local Caledonian Society's Burns Night dinner. We took with us on board the aircraft the haggis, a piper and plenty of whisky; it was a splendid occasion.

By the time I arrived at Kinloss the station had already received the last of the new Nimrods which replaced the old piston-engined Shackletons. Since the technology of the new jet aircraft and its weapons systems represented a quantum leap over that of the Shackletons, I suspect the C-in-C sent me there because, as a fighter pilot, I would have no previous knowledge of maritime operations and would therefore be asking fairly basic questions whilst the aircrews and engineers got to grips with their new machines. In particular we had to avoid doing something 'because we always did it that way'. This philosophy only works if the station commander's immediate subordinates on the operational side are themselves experts in the role, as indeed they were, so that they could provide good advice and keep the show running whilst the new man settled in.

For the first few weeks I found myself spending far too much time annoying the operations room staff by asking idiot questions. I decided that what was needed was a briefing every morning at the beginning of the day, 8.00 am, to tell me what happened the day before, what went wrong and why, and of course what was going to happen today. The briefing would begin with a summary of the weather, very much the same as we get on today's TV forecasts, which would be followed by operations, intelligence, engineering and so on. This would give me the opportunity to ask, for example, why an aircraft was late taking off the day before. The answer might be for any number of reasons involving staff from any of the three wings, so representatives from the wings and squadrons would be present to provide the answers. In discussing the contents of this chapter with one of the officers who was with me at the time, he wrote:

> I remember well your introducing the 8 am briefing which initially went down like a lead balloon, but was soon accepted by most people as essential in the jet age we had just entered. There was one amusing aspect of it which was possibly not apparent to you. The talking clock would count down the time to 8 am in 5-second intervals prior to your arrival at the Ops Room. You invariably arrived just as the clock was announcing 'the time is 8 am exactly'. Among the station execs you were famous for your precise timing and we all did our best to be seated in the Ops Room well before your arrival, as none of us wanted to suffer the indignity of being locked out. Quite often however, someone would arrive just after you to find the door to the briefing room had been locked. There would follow a panic-stricken shaking of the door handle much to the quiet amusement of those safely in the room. Sitting in the front row you would not have noticed the people behind hurriedly scanning the scene to discover which squadron had an empty chair. This was no more than a mild bit of inter-squadron rivalry and we'd usually deduced the name of the poor devil locked outside by the end of the met briefing. As I remember, my squadron were the worst offenders.

After the initial resistance to this extra chore which I had introduced, I noticed more and more people attending the briefing because they too realised that they had not previously been brought fully into the picture. After a short time they wondered how they had got on without it.

On one occasion our Mountain Rescue Team had been called out to look for a missing German climber who had been climbing by himself, and who had not returned from a day in the Cairngorms. The following morning the team leader told us at the briefing that they had been searching the area when some others joined in to help. One of them turned to the leader and said, 'Und who are ve lookink for?' It was him.

Having been used to very precise timing in the fighter world I was surprised when there appeared to be no great sense of urgency in aircraft taking off exactly at the planned time. This was because if the crew were aiming to enter their operating area at a particular time 1,000 miles away, they could easily make up time by flying there a bit faster if they were late departing. This was true, but the downside was that all those involved in preparing the aircraft thought that it didn't much matter if it took off ten minutes late or fifteen or whatever, and a sense of urgency seemed to be lacking. I therefore introduced the policy of aircraft taking off exactly on time, measured by releasing the brakes at the beginning of the take-off run exactly to the second. I think they all thought I was mad and I actually got ticked off by a staff officer from Group Headquarters at Northwood. But it worked. In no time aircraft captains were making it a point of honour to be exactly on time and this sense of urgency fed right back through the system to the supply clerk who had to find a spare part in a hurry, to the engineer who had to fit it and the aircrew who had to drive the aircraft and so on.

This policy subsequently paid off during the Falklands War when our Nimrods flew out of Ascension Island, some 3,300 miles north of the Falklands. The only way they could operate was by refuelling in flight. The detachment commander gathered together the ground crew to explain in detail why a Nimrod on a flight- refuelled mission had to depart exactly on time even if the crew had to transfer to the standby aircraft. It hadn't occurred to them that the Nimrod had to meet the Victor tanker, which was already airborne, at a precise time and place, and that superhuman efforts were to be the norm.

Our headquarters were in Edinburgh and I answered to the Commander of the Northern Maritime Air Region, an Air Vice-Marshal who also held the appointment of 'Air Officer Scotland'. He had a splendid official residence outside Edinburgh and he and his wife hosted many delightful lunches. At one of these the main course was a superb soufflé. Our hostess asked the steward to bring the soufflé back to offer second helpings to the guests, but after a short pause a very embarrassed steward returned from the kitchen to say that the chef had eaten it – we thought this was hilarious, but our hostess was not amused.

All operational RAF stations within NATO were subject to periodic no-notice 'TACEVALS', or Tactical Evaluations. A team of NATO officers would arrive at some ungodly hour, unannounced, and pitch us into a simulated wartime situation, perhaps by saying that our operations room had been blown up and then setting us a typical task which would include preparing all possible aircraft to be serviceable for flying. Everyone was alerted by sirens blowing throughout the camp and the married quarter area; those living off the camp would be telephoned. We would all dress very hurriedly and report for duty within minutes of hearing the alarm. These were exciting exercises, and most of us enjoyed them, but they were the main way the operational effectiveness of the station was judged by our Commander-in-Chief, so there was a very serious side to them.

As part of a TACEVAL our security officer used to periodically call an exercise which involved an 'intruder' who might be someone from outside the station and who would not therefore normally be recognised, and who would be given a false identity card with incorrect details. On one occasion the security officer, who was a tall, well-built man, gave his card to a very short thin 'intruder'. The guard at the entrance to our headquarters building failed to notice that the card said the owner was 6 ft 6 inches tall and said to the short intruder, 'That's funny, you've got the same name as our security officer – OK mate, in you come.' If he had even compared the photograph on the card with the intruder he would have noticed a marked difference.

Quite apart from TACEVALs, all stations were, and still are, subject to an annual inspection by the Air Officer Commanding (AOC). All aspects of the station are examined, much of the work being done by the various staffs visiting beforehand and examining each section before reporting to the AOC. He then has a good idea of what he is looking for. During our second year the AOC came up the day before, arriving late afternoon, for a dinner party which we had arranged for him in our house. I met him at the aircraft and drove him to Langcot House. Soon after arriving he handed me his DJ trousers and said, 'Please ask your man to press these.' We didn't have a 'man', although we did have an excellent civilian housekeeper, but she had the afternoon off prior to helping us with the dinner party. The AOC never found out that his trousers were pressed by his station commander.

A conventional RAF operational station is organized with three wings – operations, engineering and administrative – each commanded by a wing commander. I was particularly fortunate in that my three wing commanders were first class and I knew I could rely on them wholeheartedly. In fact we became very good friends with them and their families and now, thirty-five years later, we are still very much in touch although we are all beginning to creak a bit.

Soon after I arrived I was appointed as ADC to the Queen, one of about ten RAF officers honoured in this way at any one time. It carries no extra responsibilities, but it does entitle us to wear the Queen's cypher (EIIR) on the shoulders of our uniforms and to wear aiguillettes on appropriate occasions. Needless to say, it is a great honour to be selected in this way.

For me, one of the attractions of service life is that it is a very fast-changing world, with new challenges to be met on every posting. I soon realized I had a great deal to learn about this new role and indeed was still learning when I left Kinloss two years later. By contrast, I pity some of my civilian friends who have stayed in the same job for years on end.

When the Royal Navy lost its aircraft carriers in the 1960s the fleet lost its AEW facility which was provided by carrier-borne Fairey Gannets. These aircraft could detect low-flying enemy aircraft which could not be seen beyond the horizon by ships' radars. There was also a need to detect low-flying enemy aircraft well beyond the range of land radars. This facility is now provided by Boeing E-3 Sentry aircraft, a development of the 707 airliner, but before these aircraft became available, the Shackletons were resurrected by fitting them with the same radar which the Gannets had previously used. Twelve aircraft were modified to become the Shackleton AEW Mk 2 and the new squadron, No. 8, arrived at Kinloss in 1971. No. 8 Squadron had been in Aden flying Hunters during my time there, but it was disbanded prior to the formation of the new Shackleton squadron, which adopted its number.

The Shackleton was a noisy, uncomfortable aircraft and there were some pessimists who said the new squadron would have a morale problem. Admittedly the aircraft had gained a few nicknames during its earlier life such as 'The Growler', '10,000 Rivets Flying in Loose Formation', 'The Flying Spark Plug' and 'The Contra Rotating Nissen Hut'. But these were names of affection and I soon found that the morale on 8 Squadron was commendably high as they took to their new role. I persuaded their commanding officer that their station commander really ought to know how to fly their aircraft and, after some dual-control instruction from the training officer, Squadron Leader David Green, I was sent 'solo' for a short flight with a small volunteer crew. At least I think they were volunteers. Many years earlier I had flown a Lancaster which, from a handling point of view, was somewhat similar. Nevertheless I was particularly proud to be able to add this venerable aircraft to my log book.

One of the ways a station commander gets to know his officers and their families is by entertaining and our visitors book shows that we enjoyed the

With Squadron Leader David Green, right, after my first solo in a Shackleton.

company of about 2,000 visitors to Langcot House during out two-year tour. Altogether there were 2,500 RAF and civilian personnel working on the station, together with their families amounting to another 2,000 living in the married quarters. When I arrived about 200 were officers and I decided that the only way I was going to learn all their names was to have a rogues gallery stuck on the back of the loo door. This worked well and after a few months I thought I knew everyone. I found I could cope with learning 200 names, but when 8 Squadron arrived with another 100 officers I never managed to master the names of all 300.

Kinloss has one of the best weather factors of any airfield in the British Isles. During our two years there we only lost one day when the weather was too bad for flying, and that was due to the 'Haar', a sea fog which used to roll in. Normally the Haar would obligingly stop when it got to the runway, a mile or so from the coast of the Moray Firth, but on this occasion it kept going. Due to our excellent weather there were many occasions when aircraft would deploy to Kinloss for a few days whilst the weather down south was too bad for flying. This particularly applied to some of the training aircraft when there was a risk of a course becoming unacceptably delayed by bad weather. These visitors were always warmly welcomed.

There is a good indoor swimming pool which was given to the station by the Nuffield Trust, a charity donating welfare facilities which cannot be provided from the public purse. Thereafter public money must not be used for the maintenance of these facilities and the unit must therefore raise sufficient funds to keep them going. Unfortunately we ran out of money in the fund which maintained the pool and we could not afford to keep it open during the winter of 1972. The girls and boys of the Kinloss Senior Swimming Club then said that if they raised the money, would I keep the pool open? Naturally I agreed, whereupon they ran a very effective campaign with a sponsored swim. These children, each accompanied by an airman, visited all the sections on the station seeking sponsorship and when a young girl called in to see me in my office I said I would gladly sponsor her for £1 a length. The airman with this young lady interrupted and said, 'Sir, I think I should warn you that each of these children intend to swim 50 lengths.' I quickly downgraded my offer.

On the day, I thought it would be a bit of fun if I opened the event by diving into the pool and swimming the first length fully-clothed in my uniform. This I did and I rather foolishly set off in a fast crawl to complete a length. By the time I was halfway along the pool I was exhausted by the weight of my waterlogged uniform and only just managed to reach the far end. I dragged myself out of the water and felt dreadful. I then realized that this might have been some sort of a warning that I had reached my limit and, now that I was in my forties, I could not do all that I had done in my twenties. At the end of the event the children gave me a delightful present of an engraved and mounted

Six lanes but only one winner.

silver dice, pointing out that there may have been six lanes in the pool, but that there was only one winner. They raised over £500 and the pool remained open throughout the winter.

HRH the Prince of Wales, who was learning to fly at Cranwell, visited us to fly in a Nimrod. He flew up as a Flight Lieutenant in a Jet Provost, accompanied by his flying instructor, Flight Lieutenant Dick Johns who later became Chief of the Air Staff and is now Governor of Windsor Castle. Prince Charles visited a number of stations at that time to learn about the operational capability of the RAF. HRH was met by the Lord Lieutenant, Captain Iain Tennant, and stayed the night with us at Langcot House where we had a supper party for him to meet representative officers and their wives. It was a very happy occasion.

In 1972 I was asked to take a Nimrod to India in the hope that they might want to buy some. I was very pleased to do so, although I personally did not think it was a good idea because I felt it was not the right aircraft for them. We took with us a very high-powered team from British Aerospace, the makers of the

Flight Lieutenant H.R.H. the Prince of Wales visited RAF Kinloss and is welcomed by the Lord Lieutenant of Morayshire, Iain Tennant.

Nimrod, which included the aircraft's chief designer. Our first call was to Delhi to brief their military and intelligence staffs. We were then asked to fly to Poona and, before landing, to carry out an operational demonstration. I explained that we had an engineering support team with us and could not give justice to the operational capability of the Nimrod if we had passengers and equipment getting in the way of the operators in the rear of the aircraft. I said that if the Indian Air Force could fly our support team to Poona in one of their transport aircraft, of course we would be delighted to show them what the Nimrod could do. I expected them to use one of their Hawker Siddeley 748s which they were building under licence, so you can imagine my surprise when, the following morning, I arrived at the airport to see a Russian AN 12 (NATO code named 'Cub') alongside our Nimrod.

The AN12 is similar to our Hercules in appearance, but I soon realized it was a very different aircraft. I asked if I could fly in the AN12 to Poona, and after seeking agreement from their head of intelligence, an Air Commodore, I met the aircraft's captain, an Indian Air Force Squadron Leader. I was delighted when he allowed me to sit in the first pilot's seat and I flew the aircraft all the way except for the take-off and landing. The impression I got of the AN12 was that it was an extremely rugged aircraft and easy for a third world country to maintain, although I was interested to see that there were no seat belts for the passengers, only for the flight deck crew. When I commented on this to the Squadron Leader he said that they had only had one accident with their AN12 and seat belts would not have helped them on that occasion. All the instruments were metric and dymo tape labels were stuck on whenever translations from the Russian were necessary. I noticed four large buttons just above the windscreen labelled 'Disfeathering Buttons'. From a handling point of view I thought the ailerons were incredibly heavy, despite the fact that there was anhedral on the outer wings. I have often wondered whether I was the first RAF officer to fly a Russian aircraft in support of an RAF operational mission.

While we were in India our British Aerospace team visited the factory at Bangalore where the 748s were being built. This was the same type as the RAF's Andover. The team told me the following day that they were astonished to see that the Indians were building a better aircraft than was being produced in Manchester, and not a single representative from Manchester was there to advise.

Our relations with the local community at Kinloss were excellent and we made many good friends amongst them. Luckily most of our flying was over the sea so, apart from taking off and landing, we caused little trouble. I remember asking the Provost (Mayor) of Forres, our nearest town, whether he received many complaints about aircraft noise. He replied that the only noise he heard was the noise of his cash register – he was very conscious of the fact that our airfield, and also the Royal Navy's airfield nearby at Lossiemouth, made an enormous financial contribution to the county. The Navy was operating Buccaneers and they often flew over the land which occasionally upset the locals. One of them rang up Lossiemouth to complain about a very low-flying Buccaneer; he even managed to get the number of the aircraft and said on the phone, 'And what's more I know I hit it with my son's bow and arrow and if you check up you will find that this is so.' Needless to say the aircraft, which by now had landed, was quickly checked and to everyone's astonishment there was an arrow with a suction pad stuck on the side of the fuselage. It was, of course a set-up, but we all had a good laugh about it.

We were particularly proud to have been awarded the Wilkinson Sword of Peace for 1971. These awards were made annually by the sword makers, to a unit of each of the three services, for outstanding efforts to foster good relations with the community in which it served. The work of our Mountain Rescue Team obviously was an important element in our favour and I received the award on behalf of the station in July from the Duke of Edinburgh at a ceremony at the Festival Hall in London. Two days later we were able to display the Sword to the public at an open day where we were able to raise some £2,500 for charity. We were keen to be able to raise enough money to buy a mini-bus for the retirement home in Forres after we discovered that some of the residents were never able to get away for local visits. The money raised at

On behalf of RAF Kinloss I received the Wilkinson Sword of Peace for 1971 from the Duke of Edinburgh at the Festival Hall.

our Open Day just about covered the cost of a brand-new Ford Transit which we subsequently presented to Provost Forbes after the ceremony of Beating the Retreat in Forres. We also raised enough money to form a trust, the Forres Osprey Trust, to pay for the running of the mini-bus.

Soon after I arrived I was told that if I received an invitation from Forres Town Council to test the water at the local reservoir a few miles to the south of the station, I must under no circumstances decline it. Sure enough this mysterious invitation arrived and together with the councillors and other invited guests we visited the reservoir. We were all very serious while we tasted samples of the water and made all the right noises about its excellence – then the whisky bottles came out.

On a regular basis I used to invite local residents and organizations to visit the station in the evenings so that I could tell them what we were about in the hope that they would feel that their taxes were being well spent. I would start off with a slide show giving the history of the station and telling our guests all about our operational role. They were then invited to the crew room of one of the squadrons for coffee and a chat to the officers and NCOs. This proved to be a very good PR exercise. Close to the station was the Findhorn Community which was formed in 1962 and, according to its website, 'The Findhorn Community is an example of an unintentional community which grew out of the spiritual impulse of its three founders and which has now evolved into a demonstration of blending spirituality and ecology'. Thinking they might have been pacifists and would not be happy with a major military unit on their doorstep, I therefore decided to invite them to one of our evening visits to explain that we were part of the deterrent and that we were therefore in existence to *prevent* war, but to have the capability to wage it if the deterrent failed. It is this capability which gives meaning to the deterrent. I was very surprised, and greatly encouraged, when the leader of the group stood up to thank me at the end of my presentation and said they were grateful for our presence because military units such as ours maintained the freedom that enabled communities such as theirs to carry out their experiments.

I also had a good liaison with Gordonstoun School which was quite close to Kinloss. I was keen for members of their Cadet Force to visit us and, if possible, to fly with one of the squadrons so was surprised that they had not taken up my offer after a number of invitations. I found it difficult to believe that their young people would not enjoy such a visit and when I tried to find out why they were not coming, I discovered that my invitations were being blocked by one or more of the teachers who were perhaps of a left-wing or pacifist tendency. However, after a group of teachers attended one of my evenings the boys and girls began to visit and I felt very honoured to be subsequently invited to address the school at their Remembrance Sunday inter-faith service.

While we were at Kinloss the Royal Navy left nearby Lossiemouth and handed the station over to the RAF. I was invited to their final guest night in the Ward Room, a splendid affair with several of the previous captains also present. I am proud of the fact that after the dinner I was thrown to the ground by an Admiral of the Fleet, the top rank in the Navy. During the dinner a young lieutenant, who had blotted his copybook by ditching one of their aircraft when it ran out of fuel, set off a thunderflash which had been placed in a cabbage mounted on a flower pedestal. This was quite funny at first because, for the next few minutes, everyone was trying to pick minute specs of cabbage off their mess kit uniforms. Unfortunately he kept on doing it and by then it was no longer amusing. I was talking to Admiral of the Fleet Sir Caspar John (son of the artist Augustus and who was the first aviator to become First Sea Lord) in the bar after dinner when he spotted the phantom bomber just behind me. Quite suddenly the Admiral grabbed me by the lapels of my jacket and threw me down. A moment later the thunderflash went off very close to where my ear would have been. I will always be grateful to that very distinguished officer.

Immediately before handing over command of the station to Group Captain George Chesworth, who later became Lord Lieutenant of Morayshire, I carried out my last flight in a Nimrod as the aircraft captain with my Wing

Handing over command of RAF Kinloss after my last flight.

Commander Operations, Wing Commander 'Mo' Short, as my co-pilot. For both of us this was a symbolic occasion and a fitting finale to my two years as station commander.

For many RAF officers, commanding a station is the peak of their ambitions. It is analogous to a sailor wanting to be captain of his ship, or a soldier wanting to command his regiment. Any further promotion may well bring interesting

Wg Cdr 'Mo' Short accompanied me as co-pilot on my last flight in a Nimrod immediately before handing over command of the station.

and exciting appointments, but they are not so likely to be in direct contact with the front-line weapons systems or the people who operate and maintain them. Thus our two years at Kinloss proved to be one of the most rewarding and happy two years of my career.

Chapter 14
Thinking Time

After I left Kinloss I was fortunate enough to be selected to attend the 1973 course at the Royal College of Defence Studies (RCDS), held at Seaford House in London's Belgrave Square. As previously mentioned, I had never regarded myself as being in any way intellectual and my selection therefore came as a great surprise, but a very welcome one. In explaining what lay ahead for me I can do no better than to quote from the college website:

The Royal College of Defence Studies

The Royal College of Defence Studies is an internationally renowned institution and component of the United Kingdom's National Defence Academy. It is committed to achieving its mission in an invigorating environment, which inspires study, stimulates thought and stirs debate; in which the views of others are respected and lasting friendships made; and which, through contact and exchange of information and ideas amongst members from many nations and different backgrounds, provides a unique and enriching experience for all.

The RCDS Mission is

To prepare senior officers and officials of the United Kingdom and other countries and future leaders from the private and public sectors for high responsibilities in their respective organisations, by developing their analytical powers, knowledge of defence and international security, and strategic vision.

The College used to be known as the Imperial Defence College, the IDC, but by 1971 'Imperial' had become a dirty word so the College joined the politically correct world by changing its title to RCDS. There were seventy-five of us on the 1973 course, most of whom were the rank of colonel or brigadier (and the equivalent in the other services or civilian organizations), with a fascinating mix of personalities. About half the students were British and half were from foreign or Commonwealth countries. Fellow students included, amongst others, a Japanese professor, an American CIA man, an Italian diplomat, a Nigerian general, an Iranian brigadier, a Malaysian air vice-marshal, an Australian group captain, a Kenyan brigadier, an Indian naval captain, a German general, a Turkish brigadier and a French Air Force colonel. The Japanese professor spoke good English having studied in the USA and took notes on the lectures in English, then in the evening painstakingly translated everything into Japanese script. Initially he was very formal and correct, always bowing on the first meeting of the day, but one lunchtime he greeted me at the bar, this time without a bow, and said, 'Have a drink John.' He had got the message at last.

The course studied military and political international affairs together with their sociological and scientific implications. Lectures and seminars took place in the morning and the afternoons were usually free. Most of us had led very busy lives by the time we arrived on the course and had not recently had much chance to do any serious studying, or even thinking. These free afternoons gave us the chance to follow up any ideas we might have had in the past and to develop them using the excellent library and the advice of a very knowledgeable librarian to point us in the right direction. One of the major tasks of the course was to produce a 10,000-word thesis on any subject, provided it involved defence, however remote. As a committed Christian I had for some time been interested in the so-called Just War and how this can be reconciled with the Bible which tells us 'to turn the other cheek', so I decided to write a thesis which I called 'Should a Christian Take up Arms?' My problem was to resist the temptation to write the conclusion first and then spend the rest of the paper trying to justify it. My worry was that if I came to the wrong conclusion, I might have had to resign. Much to my surprise my thesis was one of twelve selected for publication in the 'Seaford House Papers' which are filed in the College library.

We were fortunate enough to be flown over to visit the Paris Air Show which alternates each year with the one at Farnborough. Sadly this was the show when the Soviet Tu-144 supersonic airliner crashed in full view of the spectators. Popularly known as the 'Konkordski' because of its remarkable similarity to Concorde, it had been displayed throughout the week after the Concorde display and it was generally thought that the Soviet pilot was trying to outdo the British one. Having served on several boards of inquiry investigating aircraft crashes I am well aware that different so-called expert witnesses can give varying impressions of what they think they have seen. Although I still have a very clear idea of what I thought I saw, I accept that I may have been wrong. My impression was that the Tu-144 pilot pulled up to do a 'wingover' and allowed the nose to drop too far so that he found himself in

The Tu-144 taxying out on its last flight with Concorde overhead.

a very steep nose-down attitude at a height when it would have been unlikely that he could have recovered. He did the only possible thing in that he tried to pull out of the dive, but over-stressed the aircraft and the left wing came off with the inevitable tragic results. I thought at the time that this was a clear case of pilot error.

There are a number of interesting websites which report on this accident and there appears to be no clear explanation. One story is that a French Mirage fighter took off from a neighbouring airfield with the intention of filming the movement of the TU-144's 'canards', small retractable wings just aft of the cabin which are used in subsonic flight. One Soviet report said that the pilot tried to take avoiding action on suddenly seeing the Mirage and pulled up too steeply so that the aircraft stalled, resulting in the steep nose-down attitude. I did not see a Mirage, but realize that it may well have been there. Another theory is that, shortly before the last fatal flight, the Soviet ground engineers had made changes to the auto-stabilization input to the flying controls, with the intention of giving the pilot better manoeuvrability so that he could outfly Concorde, but that they had accidentally wired up the system incorrectly so that the aircraft went into a steeper climb than the pilot intended. At first it was reported that the black box had been destroyed, but some time later the Russians admitted that they had secretly removed it, so they probably know the answers but have not published them.

I have my own thoughts on the subject of flying displays. In the days when I carried out many low-level aerobatic displays with both jet and piston aircraft, I never felt completely satisfied unless I was able to practise regularly, perhaps three or four times shortly before each event. Furthermore, it is a golden rule that, having finalized a routine, you do not ad lib during the display itself and try to do something you had not fully rehearsed. I am sure that it is difficult for test pilots of jet airliners to get the opportunity to practise their display routine as often as they would wish, so perhaps they should probably not be too ambitious in planning it.

There are several other factors which I think may be significant. Most military aircraft, particularly fighters, have very good visibility from the cockpits. Airliners on the other hand mostly have poor visibility in that they have a roof over the pilot's head and a relatively narrow field of vision through the windscreens, so that it is not unusual for a pilot of these aircraft to become disorientated when in an extreme attitude which he is not used to. I actually witnessed an incident when I was watching our Nimrod display pilot practising his display routine at Kinloss. This was being filmed which is usually done so that the pilot can be comprehensively debriefed after the flight. In this instance the pilot pulled up to do a wingover, very similar to what I thought I saw with the Tu-144, but he let the nose drop too far and consequently had to pull beyond the g limit in recovering. Luckily there was no structural damage, but there was a very surprised pilot when he saw the film – he had absolutely no idea he had allowed the aircraft to get into such an extreme attitude. Could this have happened to the Tu-144 pilot? During flying training I believe learning how to do competent aerobatics is essential, even if the embryo pilot's ambition is to become an airline pilot. Many airline pilots, at least once in their career, have been faced with an unfamiliar extreme aircraft attitude, perhaps caused by excessive turbulence or an auto-pilot malfunction. He is, in my opinion, less likely to become disoriented in his flight deck with a limited view, and he would be more likely to take the correct recovery action quickly if he had been properly trained in aerobatics. But then, as an aerobatic enthusiast, I would say that, wouldn't I?

Shortly after I wrote the above paragraphs I read Stepan Mikoyan's very interesting Memoirs (Stepan Anastasovitch Mikoyan, *Memories of Military Test-flying and Life with the Kremlin's Élite*, p. 354). He was the nephew of Artem Mikoyan who had designed many of the MiG fighters; Stepan was himself a distinguished test pilot of most of them. He wrote:

> I would like to say a few words about one of the air disasters of the century – the fatal accident of the Soviet supersonic liner Tu-144 at the Bourges Salon in 1972 [it was actually in 1973]. There are two or three aspects of that accident which I will mention here. The main cause of the crash was the pull-up manoeuvre which the pilots attempted to do in imitation of their foreign colleagues. This manoeuvre had never been performed in the Tu-144 before. The pilot himself, Mikhail Kozlov, was not experienced in it either; if he had ever done it at all, it would have been only as a student, for he was

a bomber pilot and would not do any aerobatics in his normal job. On finding himself in an unusual position with the horizon hidden behind the nose of his machine, Kozlov must have pushed the wheel too hastily and too far, overshooting in pitch. The Tu-144 was a tailless aeroplane and as such would be extremely sensitive to pushing the control column forward. It reacted to Kopzlov's aggressive push on the column by rotating sharply from a climb to a vertical dive. And then another factor came into play. As was seen from the video footage, the pilot delayed the pull-out from the dive by a couple of seconds. It has been assumed that the delay was caused by the video camera that was dropped by the cameraman (he was sitting between the two pilots) and landed between the pilot's seat and the control column. It could be so, but I believe there is a more plausible explanation. The negative G load which accompanied the sharp vertical dive would have tossed the pilot up from his seat – it has been said that Kozlov was not properly strapped in – and at this moment he would have unconsciously have pressed on the wheel, thus pushing it further forward instead of pulling it. Even with the other pilot's help he would have lost one or two seconds to settle back in and start pulling the control column.

Finally, one last thing. When you are diving plumb downwards, the ground always seems to be closer than it really is, even if you are a fighter pilot who is used to such manoeuvres. To someone like Mikhail Koslov, who would have seen the ground from such an attitude for the first time, it must have seemed even closer. As soon as he had recovered his seat he might have pulled the column back with too much force and exceeded the design G-load limit of his machine. His wing disintegrated as a result, whereas if he had pulled more gently, just balancing the G-load limit, but not exceeding it, he might have had a chance to recover, even though he was indeed very near the ground.

Great minds think alike.

Towards the end of the RCDS course the students broke up into parties of a dozen or so to spend a month travelling to various parts of the world. My first choice was to go to South America because I had never been there, however I got my second choice, the Middle East, where we were due to visit Israel, Jordan, Cyprus, Turkey, Greece and Yugoslavia. This proved to be a fascinating experience. Other groups visited South America, the USA and Canada, the Indian subcontinent and the Far East.

Prior to our departure on these tours we were given a series of lectures concerning the countries we were going to visit. I was particularly interested in the Arab-Israeli situation and was rather surprised by the very pro-Arab line taken by the Foreign Office lecturers. Having spent two years with the likelihood of being shot at by Arabs in Aden, and being a typically rebellious Brit, I and several others reacted to these lectures by becoming more sympathetic to the Israelis. However, after visiting Israel I changed my mind and felt they were all as bad as each other. We were taken to one of the Israeli settlements in the West Bank and told that they were temporary, which was clearly nonsense. These very permanent-looking estates had been built on Arab territory which had been occupied after the Six Day War in 1967. The Arabs had been given no compensation and we saw Isreali maps which showed the occupied territories as being an integral part of Israel. Furthermore the senior Israeli officers who were our guides were incredibly arrogant when referring to Arabs or their problems. We visited a kibbutz on the banks of the Sea of Gallilee, which was very interesting, and we had 'Peter's Fish' for lunch. The River Jordan was a disappointment – I had always imagined it as a large fast-flowing river, but it was nothing of the sort. Jerusalem was, of course, fascinating, but we were conscious of the ever-present conflict of Arab versus Jew. It is an extraordinary city, being the centre of three of the world's greatest religions.

We viewed the occupied territories from the Golan Heights, which had been captured from Syria, because of their commanding view over Israeli-held territory. From a military point of view it seems unlikely that the Heights would ever be returned to Syria as long as the present political climate continues. We were told that Egyptian and Syrian troops were assembling on their borders, but that these were only exercises and did not represent an immediate threat to Israel. A few days after we returned home the Yom Kippur war started, so Israeli intelligence was not as good as they thought they were.

We then visited Jordan, but if you had an Israeli stamp in your passport it was not possible to visit any other Arab country – we all therefore had two passports, one for Israel and the other for the rest of the world. There was no crossing point permitted between Israel and Jordan, and although we drove to the Hussein Bridge over the river bordering the two countries, we were not allowed to cross it and therefore had to travel to Jordan all the way round via Egypt – with our second passport of course.

We visited the Baqa Palestinian Refugee Camp, which was a sad place. The striking thing about the camp was that it seemed to be overrun by children, yet there was no family planning advice available. In Amman we were briefed by Prince Hassan, King Hussein's brother and Crown Prince. We were most impressed by his grip on Jordan's political, economic and military situation and were led to believe that he was the brains behind the throne. He seemed to complement perfectly King Hussein's charismatic leadership.

From Jordan we flew to Turkey and the most memorable events were our visits to the Gallipoli battlefield and Ephesus. We stood where the Turks

The Baqa Refugee Camp in the Lebanon.

defended the peninsular against the Allied landings and could see how easy it must have been for them to direct fire down onto the troops struggling ashore below. It was still possible to pick up evidence of the campaign like the odd rifle bullet case. The beautiful city of Ephesus always impresses those who visit it for the first time. Many years later my wife Katharine and I visited the site on a Swan Hellenic cruise. Swan Hellenic had just been taken over by P & O and this was the first cruise under the new umbrella. One of the other passengers was the P & O director responsible for such cruises who had his young daughter, aged about six, with him. She was the only child on the cruise and had become quite a favourite amongst the passengers. On our arrival at Ephesus she took one look at it before bursting into tears, much to everyone's concern. When her parents asked what the matter was she simply said, 'It's all broken.'

Then on to Cyprus. We were privileged to have audiences with both the Greek President, His Beatitude Archbishop Makarios, and the Turkish Vice-President, Rauf Dentkash. We were surprised to see how short Makarios was

JS on the left with Makarios in Nicosia.

and when he sat down we saw that he even wore high-heeled shoes beneath his cassock. Shortly after we returned home Makarios was deposed in a Greek government-sponsored coup and for a short time he was in exile in London. The Turks responded by invading the north, subsequently declaring it as the Turkish Republic of Northern Cyprus. There is no doubt that the Turkish community had been treated badly by the Greek community, but the fact that no other country in the world, to date, recognizes the North as a Turkish state surely suggests that the Turkish occupation is illegal.

Our next port of call was to Greece where the highlights for me were to see the Acropolis and those extraordinary monasteries perched high on pinnacles of rock at Meteora. We had the luxury of being flown there in Greek Air Force helicopters which saved us some energetic climbs.

So far it must sound as if we were simply on a very expensive tourist trail and although to some extent this was true, but at the same time there really was a serious side to our visits. In each country we were met and briefed at the highest level on the political, military and economic situation, sometimes by our ambassador himself. As well as visits to the popular sites, we also visited many military establishments.

Our final destination was Yugoslavia where the ambassador explained to us the complicated political situation. He forecasted very accurately what he thought would eventually happen – and unfortunately it did. In 1998, twenty-five years after our visit, Serbian forces, led by Milosovic, carried out massive expulsions of ethnic Albanians living in Kosovo, which resulted in the NATO intervention.

Our first visit in Yugoslavia was to the very spot in Sarajevo where the Archduke Franz Ferdinand was murdered in 1914, which led to an attack on Serbia by Austria. Russia came to the help of Serbia, Germany came to the help of Austria and war was declared on France as Russia's ally. The German invasion of Belgium then brought Great Britain into the struggle. It seems almost incomprehensible that such a ghastly war could result from such an extraordinary chain of events following a relatively minor incident.

We were impressed with the medieval port of Dubrovnik, the 'Pearl of the Adriatic'. It is a World Heritage Site where no vehicles are allowed in the old city, nor are any modern signs or TV aerials permitted. Wandering round the streets really was like walking back through time. Sadly, the city was badly damaged in the recent Balkan conflict, but it is now the focus of a major restoration programme co-ordinated by UNESCO.

We also visited Mostar where there is that beautiful sixteenth-century bridge which was destroyed by the Bosnian Serbs in 1993. It was restored in 2004 and is now the only World Heritage Site in Bosnia Herzegovina.

After we returned home we had to justify our enjoyable wanderings around the world by giving group presentations to the rest of the course, so we were all able to benefit from what all the other groups had gained from their travels.

The beautiful sixteenth century bridge at Mostar before it was destroyed in 1992.

Our group was chided for stirring up trouble, thereby bringing about the Yom Kippur War and the overthrow of Makarios.

By now the reader must be wondering what all this has got to do with 'Silvered Wings'. The truth is that during my year with the RCDS flying was never far from my thoughts and, naturally, I fervently hoped I would land a flying appointment after the course. Imagine my excitement, therefore, when I was told that I was to be promoted to Air Commodore and sent to be Commandant of the Central Flying School at Little Rissington, an appointment I had secretly coveted for some years. There are few opportunities for air commodores to fly, and this was one of them. How lucky can you get?

Chapter 15
The Central Flying School

 A little bit of history. The Central Flying School is the oldest flying school in the world having been formed in 1912, six years before the founding of the RAF itself. In 1911, Herbert Asquith, the Prime Minister, instructed the Committee of Imperial Defence to examine naval and military aviation and suggest measures to create an efficient air force. The Committee recommended the formation of the Royal Flying Corps (RFC) comprising a Military Wing, a Naval Wing, a Reserve, the Royal Aircraft Factory at Farnborough and the Central Flying School (CFS). Captain Godfrey Paine RN was appointed as the first Commandant of CFS and was informed by the First Lord of the Admiralty, Winston Churchill, that he must learn to fly within two weeks.

CFS was formed on 12th May 1912 at Upavon. Initially the primary aim was to produce combat pilots rather than aviation pilots as such, so only men who already held a Royal Aero Club Certificate were accepted for advanced training. One of the successful students on the first course was Major Hugh Trenchard who became the Senior Staff Officer at Upavon and was later to become the first Chief of the Air Staff when, on the amalgamation of the Royal Flying Corps and the Royal Naval Air Service, the Royal Air Force was formed in 1918.

On the outbreak of war in 1914 a rapid expansion took place and by the end of 1915 the policy was for pupils to do their ab initio flying with one of the reserve squadrons, and then move on to CFS or a service squadron for advanced training. A major fault at that time, highlighted by Major Robert Smith-Barry, was a lack of standardization within the RFC. He was given command of a squadron at Gosport to put his ideas into practice, including the introduction of dual controls and the 'Gosport tube' which facilitated communication between instructor and pupil. He also advocated learning how to fly the aircraft to its limits which included entry and recovery from spins.

In 1920 CFS became the Flying Instructors School, tasked with carrying out the work started by Smith-Barry at the School of Special Flying at Gosport. The training of qualified flying instructors (QFIs) is still the main role of CFS today.

The first dinner for past and present members of the staff was held in 1930 at Wittering and the following year CFS became the first RAF unit to be granted armorial bearings, the crest of a pelican representing a seat of learning and the motto 'Imprimis Praecepta' being best translated as 'Our Teaching is Everlasting'. But it was not until 1951 that the CFS Association was formed by the then commandant, Mark Selway – I was his PA at the time and found myself as the first Hon Secretary. The CFS colours, represented in the Association's tie, are green for the Army and the Salisbury Plain where the unit was formed in 1912, purple for the engineering branch of the Royal Navy which provided most of the original engineers, silver for the River Avon which flowed close to Upavon and black for the unknown future.

With this distinguished and historic background I think I can be forgiven for the tremendous pride I felt on becoming Commandant. Before taking up the appointment in February 1974 I attended a short refresher course at Leeming flying Jet Provosts, followed by a conversion course at Valley learning how to fly our advanced trainer, the Gnat. This was the time of the fuel crisis when the use of staff cars was being severely restricted. The Station Commander at Leeming was most apologetic because he was unable to give me the use of a staff car during my stay, but he did provide me with a bicycle, not any old bicycle, but a very smart one complete with an air commodore's star plate. Although this caused much amusement, I found to my surprise that I noticed much more as I cycled around the station than I would have done had I been driving a car. I have to admit, however, that I did not follow this good example once the fuel crisis was over.

This became the third time I had been posted to Little Rissington, having completed the course in 1948 and subsequently served on the staff in 1950. I always had great affection for this happy station, not just because of its role, but because it is in a beautiful part of the Cotswolds and our relations with the local community were excellent.

We were delighted with our married quarter which was a large house with a splendid garden surrounded by a Cotswold stone wall. ap Ellis House was named after Group Captain A. ap Ellis, who was the first station commander appointed in 1938 to supervise the building of the new airfield. He took a particular interest in the construction of the house which was to become his married quarter because he knew that, unless the garden was at least an acre, he would not qualify for a gardener. The boundary of the garden had already been staked out and one night he measured the area and, as he expected, it was just under the acre. He therefore craftily moved the stakes to give him the required area, and after a beautiful stone wall had been built he applied for his gardener. His application was refused on the grounds that the garden was too small so he challenged the decision and suggested that the area be measured again. He won his case and we still had a gardener thirty-six years later.

The Commandant-in-Chief meets Flt Lt Frederick with Len Hill in July 1974.

In 1960 Her Majesty Queen Elizabeth, the Queen Mother was appointed Commandant-in-Chief. Soon after I arrived I was granted an audience and it became obvious that HM was very knowledgeable and enthusiastic about CFS in general, and the Red Arrows in particular. Her Majesty had visited the station on a number of occasions and had approved the use of 'Those Magnificent Men in their Flying Machines' as our official march past.

Since a pelican is the crest on our coat of arms it was very appropriate for a live one to be our mascot. During my time as Commandant this was Flight Lieutenant Frederick who was looked after by Len Hill, the owner of 'Birdland' in Bourton-on-the-Water. Frederick used to greet important visitors and would also present his compliments to the Mess President after the loyal toast during guest nights in the Officers' Mess.

A short time after my arrival I went to the Ministry of Defence to interview four WRAF officers who had been shortlisted to become my PA. Only one, Cheryl Barber, showed any interest in flying so of course she had to be chosen, and this proved to be a very good choice. She carried out her work with great

To commemorate the departure of the Varsity from CFS, Examining Wing organized a formation of all nine CFS types which was flown over Little Rissington in October 1974. The formation was led by Flt Lt Dennis Barber in the Varsity. I flew No. 9 at the back of the formation as co-pilot to Sqdn Ldr Ken Pollard in the Dominie, the military version of the HS 125 business jet.

enthusiasm and efficiency, and even managed to find a husband before she left. Dennis was a member of our Examining Wing and we have kept in touch with them both ever since. Having held her post myself in 1951 I had some sympathy with what Cheryl had let herself in for. While not exactly part of her duties, I was grateful for the fact that she kept an eye on any interesting visiting aircraft so that she could drop the hint to me that I might like to add a new type to my log book. Consequently I managed to get my hands on some sixty-six different types, many of them civil, during this tour. When she had flown in all nine of the CFS types I presented her with the staff badge for her flying suit.

The annual reunions of past members were always interesting and enjoyable occasions. We would accommodate some of the more distinguished members in our house and would hear many tales of their past exploits. Air Commodore d'Arcy Greig, the Association President, was a regular attender – he had set a world speed record in 1927 and came third in the 1929 Schneider Trophy race flying the Supermarine S5; he also used to 'wing walk' in the early Hendon displays. Marshal of the Royal Air Force Sir Dermot Boyle, an ex-Chief of the Air Staff and Patron of the CFS Association told us of how he took the Queen Mother up on her first flight in a Puss Moth when she was the Duchess of York

Wren's splendid cartoon drawn at the 1974 CFS reunion. Aeroplane Magazine/www.aeroplanemonthly.com

and got ticked off for doing so. Mark Selway, who was Commandant when I was his PA in the 1950s told stories of how he flew in the inverted leader formations at Hendon with the Tutors, and John Oliver actually instructed during the First World War. In 1975 Sir George Edwards, the designer of Concorde, was our guest of honour – when asked, after his speech at the dinner, whether he had ever been involved with helicopters, he replied that he had spent all his energy in trying to make sure that the wings on *his* aircraft didn't move.

CFS had pioneered methods of teaching instrument flying way back in 1930 when Flight Lieutenant W.E.P. Johnson, following a civilian course in 1929 at the Farman factory in France on 'Pilotage without exterior visibility', developed a system for teaching pilots how to fly safely in cloud. To prove his point he would give demonstrations by taking off alone in an Avro 504N under a hood over the cockpit. He would then fly several aerobatic manoeuvres, including a spin, and not open the hood until he was about 200 ft from the ground on the approach to the airfield.

CFS is responsible for selecting and training the highest calibre of flying instructors and for developing, checking and maintaining the highest possible standards of pure flying and flying instruction on both fixed-wing and rotary-wing aircraft, and also of synthetic training within the RAF and, on request, the Army, the Royal Navy and many other international air forces. The

Flight Lieutenant W.E.P Johnson taking off under the hood in an Avro 504 in 1931 at Wittering to demonstrate the ability to fly on instruments. The Flight Collection

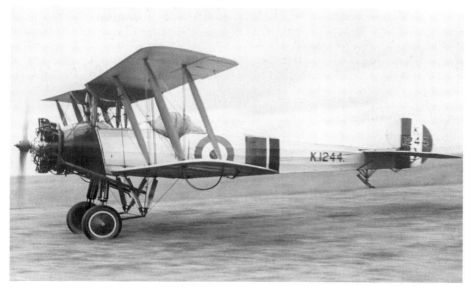

checking is carried out by the CFS Examining Wing and I had the pleasure of leading several overseas visits, either in the examining role or in a liaison capacity to exchange information with other services.

One such visit took us to Jordan where I flew with several Jordanian cadets testing them flying their American T37 jet trainers, but the highlight of that visit for me was my flight in a two-seat F-104B Starfighter. The Jordanian pilot, a major, gave me the best pre-flight briefing I have ever had and he allowed me to fly the aircraft from the front seat which was a very exciting experience.

The Lockheed F-104 was the first Mach 2 (twice the speed of sound) fighter and when it entered service in the mid 1950s it was ahead of its time. It had tiny wings of only 22 ft span and with its length of 55 ft it was popularly known as 'the missile with a man in it'. During take-off I noticed for the first time that I found myself doing 200 knots (230 mph) yet we were still on the runway. It was pleasant to fly, but while it was faster than the Lightning, it did not have the manoeuvrability of that splendid British product. The F-104 served with many air forces throughout the world, but it had a somewhat chequered career with the German Air Force when there were so many fatal accidents that it became known as the 'widow maker'. The majority of these accidents were caused by pilot error due to a number of factors. The F-104 was a very demanding aircraft to operate, and whereas most air forces used only those pilots who had already flown a tour with an operational squadron, such experienced pilots did not exist since the German Air Force was not reformed after the Second World War until 1957. They therefore had no option but to use newly graduated rather than experienced pilots. Key personnel on a military air force

A Jordanian two-seat F104. Michiel Vogelpoel

squadron are the supervisors – the flight and squadron commanders – but few of them had jet flying experience when the F-104s arrived. This combination of inexperienced pilots and inexperienced supervisors, combined with a high-performance aircraft being used in a low-level role, often in bad weather, all contributed to the high accident rate.

During our visit to Jordan I flew one of the Royal Flight Alouette helicopters from Amman to the amazing Nabataean Arab city of Petra. The initial view of the stunning Treasury building as one exits the narrow 'siq' is never to be forgotten. The 40 m high building was hewn out of the living rock in the Roman period and was not rediscovered until 1812 by the Swiss explorer Burckhardt. It was immortalized by Dean Burgen in his poem '*Petra*' when he described 'A rose-red city, half as old as time.' I have read the Treasury building described as arguably the most beautiful building in the world and I do not think that is an exaggeration.

We visited the Swedish Air Force because they had had several accidents in bad weather and they were interested in how the RAF taught instrument flying. One can easily become disorientated when flying in cloud, or even very bad visibility, when one can experience a strong sensation of, say, turning when the instruments say you are going straight and level. The essence of the training is to convince the student that the instruments, not your sensations, are telling the true story. I had a good illustration of the problem when I was instructing on Meteors. The student pilot had taken off when we flew almost immediately into low cloud. After a short time he wanted to put the aircraft into a steep dive because he was convinced we were climbing too steeply. I told him to follow his instruments, but he failed to do so. This was one of the few occasions when I had to take control of the aircraft from a student, in this case to stop it from diving into the ground. I am convinced that if he had been by himself on that occasion he might well have killed himself.

In 1968 the three separate military services in Canada were unified into a single organization, the Canadian Armed Forces, with standard green uniforms to replace the Canadian Army khaki and the Royal Canadian Air Force blue. At the time this reorganization was somewhat controversial and this was illustrated to us in an amusing way. Towards the end of a very interesting visit to Canada to discuss our flying training systems, our team was transiting through Toronto airport's terminal building when, to our astonishment, we were clapped by the public – we were in our blue RAF uniforms and could not understand why we merited such treatment. We were subsequently told that the public were not clapping the RAF, rather they thought that the RCAF had come back with their blue uniforms.

From Toronto we flew to the United States to study the American flying training organization and to tell them about the forthcoming introduction of our new advanced trainer, the Hawk. When we landed at Webb Air Force Base

Connie Edwards in his Spitfire at Webb Air Force Base.

in Texas we were surprised and thrilled to find that we were being escorted by a Spitfire which stopped on the tarmac alongside us. This turned out to be the only airworthy Spitfire in the USA at that time. It was owned and flown by Connie Edwards who invited us out to his ranch for supper that evening, when we were amazed to find that he had two hangars full of Second World War aircraft, mostly in pristine flying condition. He told us that he had done a lot of flying for films and had, in fact, organized and flown the Messerschmitt 109s from Spain for our film 'The Battle of Britain'. He was a relatively young fellow and I rather pompously asked him how many flying hours he had. I will never forget his reply, delivered in a delightful Texan drawl: 'When Ah got to 10,000 hours, Ah threw away ma log book.' And there was I, with my mere 3,500 or so hours, thinking I was the experienced one – the perfect put down.

We wondered how he had amassed his fortune so that he could buy all these wonderful aircraft and were then told that Daddy had found oil on the ranch. He was a delightful host and we much admired him.

One day in 1975 Alan (Bunny) Bramson invited me to fly a Rockwell Shrike Commander from Staverton. This is a delightful, light, twin-engine, high wing, seven-seat American business aircraft. It must surely be one of the few of its class which is cleared for aerobatics and I well remember the surprised reaction of my passengers in the back when I subjected them to a barrel roll. My overall impression was that this really was a pilot's aircraft and it was about this period that Bob Hoover gave his astonishing displays in a Shrike Commander during the SBAC shows at Farnborough. I will never forget his final manoeuvre which was to feather both propellers, loop the aircraft, carry out an eight-point roll and then land the aircraft, coming to a halt on the grass in front of the VIP enclosure. All this with both engines shut down! Bob Hoover had been a prisoner of war in Germany and escaped by commandeering a Focke Wulf FW 190. He subsequently had a brilliant career as a test pilot.

Another memorable occasion was when Neil Williams visited CFS in his Czech-built Zlin Akrobat. Neil had won the European Aerobatic Championship and was one of the few pilots at the time who knew how to fly a lomcovàk. He demonstrated this complicated and dramatic manoeuvre to me in the air, but I still do not know what we did or how he did it. The Zlin handles beautifully and is a joy to fly, although there was one famous occasion when it let Neil down. Due to metal fatigue the main spar of his port wing failed and the wing started to fold upwards. He had to think very quickly because he did not have a parachute so he couldn't bale out. He decided that if he could invert the aircraft the wing might snap back to its proper position. He was able to do this and flew back to Hullavington upside down until he was within a few feet of the ground when he managed to roll the aircraft upright as he crashlanded. Astonishingly he was unhurt, although no doubt a bit surprised. Sadly Neil, a most careful and very experienced test pilot, was killed when he was ferrying a Heinkel 111 from Spain to England.

One of the most enjoyable of my responsibilities was that of looking after the Red Arrows, then flying Gnats. I was responsible for the selection of the pilots, their supervision during training and also during the displays. The short runway at Little Rissington was not ideal for the Gnat and the local air space tended to be a bit crowded, so they operated out of Kemble about 30 miles to the south-west. I used to thoroughly enjoy flying in the back seat with each member of the team and quickly realized that not only were they superb pilots, but that they were very good representatives of the Service when away on tour.

One third of the team is new each year and they train during the winter prior to being formally cleared by the Air Officer Commanding just before the display season starts in the spring. This is followed by a press day with photographers to give the team some good publicity. Flight Lieutenant Frederick used to take part and in 1975 the press wanted to take a photograph of him briefing the team. Len Hill, Frederick's guardian, was with him and said that we must take care that there was always someone in front of him if he was facing into wind, otherwise he might take off. We did not heed his advice as well as we should have done because Frederick found a gap and he was away. It was a wonderful sight seeing him fly, but he was out of practice and not very fit so he was unable to climb out of his 'ground cushion' – then he came to a stone wall and decided that discretion was the best course and carried out a precautionary landing just in front of the wall.

One of my favourite Red Arrow photographs was taken when Dickie Duckett led the team in Viggen formation with the old Severn Bridge in the background. The formation is named after the Saab Viggen Swedish ground-attack fighter which has a similar plan form. The original idea was to take a photograph of the team from the bank of the river with the bridge in the foreground, but this did not work out. Someone then had the bright idea of positioning the photographer in a helicopter and then looping around it. This worked.

The CFS helicopters operate out of Ternhill in Shropshire and I was able to indulge my love of flying these interesting aircraft. The handling of a helicopter is quite different from flying a fixed-wing aircraft and some air forces do not allow pilots to fly both types in the same day in case they accidentally get confused. I personally found this to be nonsense and never had any difficulty in going from one to the other – after all, no one has suggested that you cannot ride a motor cycle immediately after driving a car.

CFS had been granted the freedom of Cheltenham and we often used to be invited to take part in their civic functions. I was asked by the Mayor to take the salute, jointly with him, at the disbandment parade of the local branch of the 'Old Contemptibles' – the gallant men of the British Expeditionary Force that went to war against Germany in 1914 and were referred to by the Kaiser as 'that contemptible little army'. About a dozen of these splendid old men marched immediately behind the band in an impressive parade which included the Gloucesters and all the usual ex-service and cadet organizations. I was concerned to see that the band was striding along at the full 30-inch steps at 120 paces to the minute, which seemed to me to be a bit tough on the veterans. We had tea after the parade in the Town Hall and I light heartedly joked with

The Red Arrows in Viggen formation over the old Severn bridge in 1975.

the bandmaster saying he had been a bit hard on the old men. 'Sir,' he said, 'they came to me before the parade and said, "Thirty inches at 120 to the minute or we don't go on parade."'

While at Kinloss I had been invited to become chairman of the RAF Equitation Association, which having enjoyed riding for most of my life I was delighted to accept. The Association was centred around the thriving saddle club at Cranwell; in addition there were also saddle clubs at several RAF stations. A number of serving RAF men and women had their own horses, and competitions were an important part of our ethos; apart from anything else, success in competitions provided very welcome publicity. However, I also felt that it was equally important to encourage people to ride just to enjoy the horse, even if all they wanted to do was to go for a quiet hack.

John Hamer was one of our engineering officers at Little Rissington. He and his wife Penny owned their own horses and rode very successfully. One weekend John organized a training session in the field behind ap Ellis House and he subsequently led the RAF Showjumping Team into second place in the 1974 Queen's Plate inter-service showjumping competition at the Windsor Horse Show.

Our main activity of the year was the RAF Equitation Association Championships held at Cranwell. We would host teams, not only from other saddle clubs, but also from the other armed services and the Police. There were individual classes and the usual one day combined event of dressage, cross-country and showjumping.

By 1977 I also found myself as chairman of the Combined Services Equitation Association. Our principal role was to co-ordinate the facilities of the three services so that men and women of one service could take advantage of the facilities in another. The main provider was, of course, the Army who were most co-operative in allocating places on their courses to the RN and RAF.

John and Penny Hamer demonstrate how to do it.

John Hamer (left) leading the RAF Show Jumping Team into second place in the Queen's Plate at Windsor in 1974.

Charing Cross Hospital ran a parascending club on the airfield at little Rissington at weekends. A Land Rover would tow the victims up to about 1,000 ft and they would then release their parachutes from the tow rope and carry out a normal parachute descent from that height. It was great fun, but a strange sensation being towed upwards with the canopy almost out of sight above and behind you. These parachutes had a slow forward speed through the air of about 10 mph and could be turned so that you could land into wind. They were the forerunners of the modern paraglider which is much closer to a glider than a parachute and much more manoeuvrable. Our daughter Chrissy became an enthusiast, and before she went up for the first time I persuaded her to have some training in our gym from our Physical Training Instructor (PTI) in how to land safely under different conditions. This paid off because her first landing was accidentally onto the hard concrete taxiway. With the help of the training from the PTI she achieved a perfect landing with no bruises.

We had noticed subtle changes in the Cotswold area from the time when we lived there twenty-five years earlier. So-called 'incomers' were buying the cottages that the locals could no longer afford and the nature of villages was gradually changing. This is now a widespread problem throughout the country, but we saw the seeds of it then. The Cotswolds were becoming very popular

Going up!

and there was a local saying that Bourton-on-the-Water had 'trippers', Stow-on-the-Wold had 'tourists', but Broadway had 'visitors'! There was some truth in this. We had originally thought that we would like to settle in the area, but we began to have second thoughts.

In 1975 the Ministry of Defence decided that twelve RAF stations had to close and Little Rissington was one of those chosen. While I was naturally very sad at this decision, I could not argue with it because it was more economical to develop large stations and to move smaller units into them. Little Rissington had little scope for enlargement to absorb more units because it was on the top of a hill and the relatively short runway could not be lengthened. It was simply too short for some of the fast jet aircraft to operate from safely. It seemed to me that the best option would be for a military unit, perhaps from the Army, to take over because the real estate was excellent and the locals were used to servicemen being around. Other suggestions had been an open prison – the locals would have loved that – an industrial estate or a large housing development.

Eventually it was decided that the Army would take over. Several regiments viewed the station, but they all turned it down because it was too isolated and bus services to Cheltenham were minimal. RAF personnel are used to being in remote locations and have tended to develop first-class entertainment on the station itself. Furthermore, most airmen own some form of transport so they could go for a night out if they so wished. Soldiers on the other hand were used to being based in depots in towns and they tended to make their entertainment off the base. Eventually the Adjutant General of the Army visited and he told me that the real estate was so good that he would direct a unit to move in. The 1st Battalion of the Irish Rangers was chosen.

All good things have to come to an end and after two very happy and rewarding years I was posted to Headquarters Training Command (HQTC) in February 1976. After handing over to John Sutton as Commandant, he moved to Cranwell with CFS in April when Little Rissington closed as an active flying station. The Irish Rangers then took over in September, but this proved to be a disaster for the troops and they left after only four years. Their CO is reported to have said to an RAF officer after the Irish Rangers left, 'You lucky people, the RAF wept when we left there. It is such a wonderful place to be stationed. You obviously don't understand soldiers. All they want on a night out is to get drunk, have a fight and find a woman. You can't do that in Bourton-on-the-Water.'

After the Irish Rangers left, the station became a United States Air Force Contingency Hospital in 1981, but this closed in 1984. The technical site was then converted to a business park and the domestic area was developed into a very pleasant village named Upper Rissington. The married quarters were modernized and sold and new houses were built which tastefully blended in with the earlier buildings. The airfield itself was retained by the Ministry of Defence.

Before we left we decided to give CFS a portrait of our mascot, Frederick, as a leaving present. We had recently had a superb pastel portrait done of our black Labrador 'Mr Jackson', and we persuaded the artist, Halcyon Weir, to do a similar one for Frederick. My wife Katharine took the artist to Birdland in Bourton-on-the-Water and introduced her to Frederick who was resplendent in a CFS tie. To keep his attention Katharine had to stand in a pond with a bucket of small fish which she

FLIGHT LIEUTENANT FREDERICK CFS

Flight Lieutenant Frederick, our CFS Mascot. Halcyon Weir

periodically doled out. It was a fine, but very cold day and the whole process took three or four hours. Artist and fish feeder were frozen by the end of the session, but the result was splendid.

* * *

I knew that I would be posted to a staff appointment after CFS and dreaded the prospect of going to the Ministry of Defence or having to work in London. I was therefore delighted to find myself posted to the Air Staff as 'Air Commodore Flying Training' in Headquarters Training Command at Brampton (near Huntingdon). I knew I could not expect a flying appointment and the next best thing is undoubtedly to be in a job which is associated with flying. In this instance I was responsible for the Air Staff aspects of the RAF's Flying Training organisation.

We had recently introduced the Graduate Entry Scheme whereby university graduates could enter the RAF in the rank of flight lieutenant rather than pilot officer. We became concerned that many of the graduates arriving at Cranwell for their Initial Training, particularly those with scientific degrees, were unable to express themselves properly on paper; some therefore had to have remedial English instruction. When we questioned the universities about this, we were astonished that the reply came back along the lines that they were not worried about their students not being able to write good English, all they were concerned about was that they produced ideas. What is the good of having good ideas if you are unable to express them properly on paper? 25 years later it seems to have at last become a hot issue and the newspapers have recently been making the same criticisms.

In 1978 a Royal Review was held at RAF Finningley to celebrate sixty years of the Royal Air Force. The day began with a big parade followed by a static display and then a very impressive flypast. To my horror I was appointed as deputy parade commander to Air Commodore Tony Carver – I had served with him on 26 Squadron and he was Equerry to the Queen when I was working for the Duke of Edinburgh, so I knew him well. He was based at Cranwell at the time and I just prayed that he would be fit on the day. I watched the parade from the grandstand, all dressed up with sword etc., ready to leap in if anything happened to Tony. Luckily it didn't. One of my abiding memories of the day was to see a number of very ancient retired air marshals; both they and their uniforms had clearly seen better days. I suppose I have now joined those ranks, but I am glad to say my uniform still fits – just.

The BBC were planning a programme at the time which they were going to call 'Fighter Pilot'. They intended to select four students and to follow them through all stages of basic, advanced and operational training before they became fully operational pilots on a fighter squadron. I pointed out to the team that currently only 25 per cent of those that started flying training actually reached operational status on a squadron, and that if they wanted to be sure of one of their candidates successfully completing the course they would need to select eight, not four. For understandable reasons they insisted on only selecting four, but not one of them finally became an operational fighter pilot. It was one of those occasions when I was sorry to have been proved right.

I had two happy years at Brampton flying a desk before embarking on my last appointment before retiring from the RAF.

Chapter 16
Mount Batten

I was very fortunate and also somewhat surprised to be promoted to Air Vice-Marshal for my last tour before retiring from the RAF because most officers usually retain their previous rank. My appointment was 'Commander Southern Maritime Air Region' – known in NATO language as COMSOUMAR – at RAF Mount Batten at Plymouth. I also had two war appointments with fancy NATO titles: Commander Central Sub-Area Eastern Atlantic Command and Commander Plymouth Sub-Area Channel Command. I answered to the Air Officer Commanding No. 18 Group at Northwood who had the peacetime task of 'carrying out surveillance of potentially hostile surface vessels and submarines in the Atlantic, the North Sea and home waters while attaining standards of proficiency adequate to, ensure effective maritime operations in war.'

The primary role of SOUMAR was to task and control all UK maritime air forces, and also NATO maritime aircraft, when operating out of UK bases, in an area south of a line drawn from Ireland to the tip of Greenland down to the Tropic of Cancer. The Northern Maritime Air Region, NORMAR, with its Headquarters in Edinburgh, operated north of this line.

One of my first duties on taking up my appointment was to call on the Flag Officer Plymouth, an admiral, who was my opposite number in the Royal Navy. These calls are formal occasions, but they serve a very useful purpose in that they are a quick way to get to know those with whom one will be working. I was accompanied by my ADC, an attractive WRAF officer who had been in the job some time before I arrived. As I got out of my car, dressed up in my full uniform with medals and sword, I was met by the admiral, similarly attired, whose first words were addressed to my ADC rather than to me: 'How nice to see you again, Trish' he said. I knew my place. In fact we became good friends and I greatly enjoyed working with my Royal Navy colleagues.

All our operations were joint operations with the Royal Navy. My staff and those of Flag Officer Plymouth operated from our underground Joint Operations Room at Mount Wise. We used to meet with the admiral first thing

Flying a Nimrod from St Mawgan.

each morning. The initial briefing was from the intelligence officer and I well remember his announcement in December 1979 when he told us that the Russians had just invaded Afghanistan. My initial reaction was: 'Haven't they read the history books?' The subsequent unfolding of events up to the present day is surely no surprise.

We liaised closely with the United States Navy at Lajes in the Azores and I visited them several times in a Nimrod from St Mawgan to discuss our mutual problems. Our main interest was in being able to track the movements of Soviet surface vessels and submarines operating out of their huge naval base at Murmansk.

At Mount Wise the RAF also ran the Rescue Co-ordination Centre (RCC). During a rescue operation the RCC controlled all maritime aircraft and Search and Rescue (SAR) helicopters – regardless of their nationality – operating in the SOUMAR area. They also controlled the mountain rescue teams. The RCC worked very closely with the Coastguards who were responsible for co-ordinating all surface vessels during these operations.

The RCC was run by the 'Wing Commander Operations', Wing Commander 'Min' Larkin, who gave a graphic description of how the RCC works when he wrote to me about the Fastnet Race in 1979:

I shall never forget the night of 13th/14th August. The wind and rain lashing against the windows of my married quarter that evening was a portent of what was to come. At approximately midnight the duty SAR controller at Mount Wise phoned me to report 3 yachts taking part in the annual Fastnet race were in distress, but that Land's End Coastguard had dispatched a few lifeboats to the scene. At 5am he reported that storm force 10 to 11 was blowing in the Fastnet area and as many as 30 yachts were now thought to be in trouble with an estimated 300 souls on board. As he could not cope with the constant flow of distress calls and other related communications he had called in off-duty staff to help. When I arrived at about 5:30am some half dozen staff were already working flat out to keep up with the constant demand for helicopter rescue. Initially, we used helicopters from RNAS Culdrose and RAF Chivenor, but were soon put to calling in assistance from other SAR Flights under our operational control based in other parts of the country, and also from the Irish SAR forces.

Pandemonium would be an accurate description of those first few hours in the operations room. SAR controllers struggled to keep abreast of the far-from-clear situation at sea in order to direct the available rescue helicopters to the right search areas. Helicopters were often picking up survivors from yachts which had not reported being in distress while they were on route to others which had. Keeping an accurate plot of what was actually happening in the area was difficult, to say the least. Land's End Coastguards, in overall control of the SAR operation, also had great difficulty deciphering the mass of communications on the airwaves. Eventually, however, Nimrods from RAF St Mawgan, providing invaluable assistance as top cover for the whole operation, sorted out the muddle. It would be fair to say that without the SAR expertise of the Nimrod crews the situation might have been hopeless. When the morning TV and radio news bulletins announced the rescue operation to the world we were inundated with telephone calls from anxious relatives of the 2,500 race participants. Every telephone at Mount Wise, and there were a lot of them, was continuously in use. Teleprinters in the radio room constantly spewed out streams of queries from higher authorities, the press and other interested parties. Calls came in from across the world. At one stage I was dealing with an operational matter on one phone when I was handed another to discover I was live on NZ radio, which had interrupted a commentary on an international rugby match, to get the latest news on the rescue. The most junior inexperienced staff, who normally would not be expected to parry questions from the media, became experts at it within a few hours. When it was announced that Mr Edward Heath, the Prime Minister, was taking part in his yacht, Morning Cloud, there was a media frenzy. It was a great relief in more ways than one when the Prime Minister and his crew were reported safe. For a day and a half activity in the ops room was continuous and frenetic. Many of the operations room staff remained on duty beyond their normal shift time, some working around the clock for more than 24hours. Some would just not go home. We all felt deeply for the poor souls still not located in such atrocious sea conditions. No one complained of being tired. It was an amazing example of how the mind and body copes in desperate situations.

The operation finished in the afternoon of the 15th August. By then we knew that 15 people were still missing, later confirmed dead. A total of 136 survivors were rescued by air and surface SAR forces. Happily, the vast majority of those taking part in this most challenging of sea races had weathered the storm. Feeling very tired, and not a little smelly, we drifted home to some well earned sleep. In a subsequent analysis of the incident, the 1979 Fastnet disaster was assessed as one of the biggest SAR operations in UK waters in peacetime.

A BBC programme in 2006 about that Fastnet Race gave a graphic reconstruction of some of the rescues. There was much emphasis on the excellent work of the Coastguards, but I was disappointed that, although reference was made to the co-ordinating function of the Nimrod operating overhead, no mention was made of the sterling contribution of our RCC.

Mount Batten had a long and distinguished history. During the Napoleonic Wars it had become a French prisoner-of-war camp. In 1913 a seaplane base was established and several trial flights took place. Towards the end of 1916, when the German U-boat campaign was causing great anxiety in the Western Approaches, aerial patrols were needed and RNAS Cattewater was therefore established in February 1917 with five flights of seaplanes. They carried out their escort duties with RN vessels throughout the remainder of the War. The two First World War seaplane hangars still exist today above the Cattewater slipway and are listed buildings. With the formation of the RAF in 1918, the station was renamed RAF Cattewater, but in 1922 it went into a care and maintenance basis until 1928 when flying boats and marine craft were re-introduced and the station was renamed RAF Mount Batten. Throughout the Second World War Sunderland flying boats operated out of Mount Batten and continued to do so until 1959.

In the early 1930s the station contributed to the development of high-speed craft and one of the crew members on the trials was Aircraftman T.E. Shaw

RAF Mount Batten – Plymouth.

(Lawrence of Arabia) who was stationed there under his assumed name from 1929 to 1933. Sadly he was subsequently killed in a motor cycle accident in 1935.

My own office was in the Officers' Mess overlooking Plymouth Sound. This was often considered to be the office with the best view in the RAF and I had no argument with that. My ship recognition improved greatly and I learnt much about the Royal Navy as I watched the ships come and go. In 1950 the RAF had leased Monckswood, a delightful house at Wembury, as our official residence, one which proved to be ideal for entertaining. The house was built in 1936 after the Spanish style in the estate of Wembury House. It was named after General Monck (the Duke of Albermarle), the founder of the Coldstream Guards, who owned a previous Wembury House in the 17th century.

Entertaining at home is an important part of service life for those with appointments 'in command'. At Kinloss and Little Rissington, and now at Mount Batten where I was the senior RAF officer in the South-West, we used to invite not only our own friends and neighbours, but also distinguished local residents such as the Lord Mayor, local MP, senior officers from the other services and our many official visitors to dinner and drinks parties. This most enjoyable commitment was also a helpful way of getting to know informally one's own officers and their wives – we hadn't heard about partners at that time. Luckily we had the perfect house for the job and an excellent RAF staff to help us. In return we became involved in many civic and military functions in and around Plymouth.

To assist our staff I prepared a brief to help them with the smooth running of our dinner parties when we would normally seat fourteen. Reading it twenty-five years later it seems amusingly archaic, almost as if it had come out of an early edition of Mrs Beaton's famous book, but it did enable us to concentrate on looking after our guests rather than having to supervise the staff. These dinners always seemed to work well, but I often wondered whether the staff took any notice of the brief.

Before Guests Arrive: Car Park light on. Step light on. Soft drinks prepared.

On Arrival of Guests: Receive coats and take orders for drinks. Offer to refill drinks. Remain on call in the hall.

Before Guests enter Dining Room: All candles lit. Check water glasses filled.

As Last Guest enters Dining Room: Hall lights out.

As Hostess sits down: Dining Room lights out. Offer sherry as first course is served. Remove sherry glasses with first course plates.

During Dinner: Dining Room – keep kitchen door shut. Drawing Room – clear glasses, empty ash trays, make up fires.

Main Course: Plates must be hot. Serve wine for the Air Commander to taste. Refill glasses when half empty.

The Port: Offer cigars and cigarettes after each guest has taken port. Refill port decanter immediately it has returned to the Air Commander.

As Ladies rise: Hall lights on.

After Ladies leave: The Air Commander will offer brandy to the gentlemen. Steward to take orders for liqueurs.

In the Drawing Room: Serve coffee immediately ladies enter and offer liqueurs. Serve coffee to gentlemen as they pass through the hall. Refill ladies' coffee cups. Continue to offer coffee until it is refused. Steward to hover in the hall until guests leave.

The focus of the RAF station at Mount Batten was a squadron of the RAF Marine Branch with a detachment at Tenby in South Wales; it was commanded by a squadron leader. Smaller Marine Craft Units (MCUs) at Alness in the north of Scotland, Bridlington in Yorkshire, Holyhead in Anglesey and Gibraltar were lodger units on those RAF stations. The Station

Carrying out the AOC's inspection at the Marine Craft Detachment at Tenby in South Wales.

Commander at Mount Batten was a wing commander of the Marine Branch. The twenty Marine Craft of the Branch were under the command and control of the Air Officer Commanding No. 18 Group at Northwood and the policy for the Branch was formulated by the Director of Marine Craft (DMC), a group

A Pinnace of the RAF Marine Branch.

captain, in the Ministry of Defence. However the AOC at Northwood delegated to me the responsibility of carrying out, on his behalf, the annual inspections of the station and some of the detachments. This gave me the excuse to find out all I could about the Branch and, in particular, to go to sea in the marine craft. These craft were principally used for target towing, weapons recovery, helicopter training, dingy drills for aircrew and search and rescue. During the Second World War most of the search and rescue work was carried out by the marine craft and flying boats, but that role has now been superseded by helicopters. Sadly, as one of the Government's economy measures, the Branch was disbanded in 1986 and the role taken over by civilian contractors.

My going to sea in the marine craft could give rise to a certain amount of mirth. I learnt that when two ships of the Royal Navy pass each other, the one with the junior captain has to salute the one with the senior captain. Every ship therefore carries a 'bridge card' which lists all the ships in the Service, together with the names of their captains and their seniority so that they know who has to salute whom. If we passed a ship of the RN when I was on board one of our marine craft, the Royal Navy used to play the game because the captain, usually a commander, would salute me complete with whistles blowing. No doubt there were many wry smiles on both vessels as this huge ship saluted a tiny little boat.

The formality of respecting the seniority of a ship's captain in this way possibly explains an incident that I witnessed earlier at Kinloss. We often used to fly officers of the Royal Navy, usually submariners, in our Nimrods on exercises looking for submarines. Such exchanges help with understanding each other's problems. There was an occasion when I was talking to two commanders while we watched a simulated attack on one of our own submarines at the navigator's station. Our navigator was a squadron leader and our two nautical friends could not understand why the aircraft captain, a flight lieutenant, was junior to him. I explained that the aircraft captain's rank was irrelevant. When a pilot is authorised to fly as the captain of the aircraft, regardless of the ranks of other members of the crew, the captain is in sole charge.

I have always been keen on pistol shooting and on one occasion when we were based in Germany I had won the NATO individual pistol championship. I therefore thought it would be a bit of fun if RAF Mount Batten challenged the local Royal Navy, Royal Marines and the Army teams to a competition on the range at HMS *Raleigh*, the Royal Navy's Training Establishment on the far side of Plymouth Sound. Teams were to consist of four officers. None of the other members of our team had ever done any competitive pistol shooting so we did some serious practice on the quiet at Mount Batten. I was confident that we had a good chance of winning and was delighted when we did so, much to the disgust of the Royal Marines who thought it was poor form to practise beforehand.

Katharine presents RAF Mount Batten with the Plymouth Joint Services Pistol Team Championship.

When I was instructing at Cranwell way back in the fifties I had the opportunity to do several parachute jumps when I took a party of cadets to the Parachute Training School at Upper Heyford. The opportunity repeated itself when I discovered that there is an annual event at Boscombe Down when volunteers can leap out of a Hercules into Plymouth Sound. The advantage of landing in the water is that the training time is less than for those expecting to land on hard ground. I managed to get on to one of these flights and after only a few hours training we were airborne. We jumped in pairs, one 'mature' volunteer with a younger person as the second. The first pair consisted of Major General Ken Perkins, whom I knew well from our time together at the RCDS and a young WRAF parachute packer. I was part of the second pair also with another young parachute packer. I chatted to my companion before the jump and discovered that she had jumped many times before so I told her that she could look after me rather than I should look after her. Not only had Ken Perkins never jumped before, but it was obvious that his companion was terrified. We were all very anxious about her because, if she decided not to jump, that would have a disastrous effect on the morale of the rest of us. In the event she did jump and as she was floating down close to Ken, he shouted across to her to ask if she was OK. She just held her arms out and shouted back: 'Geronimo!' One can only have great admiration for this young lass, who knew

About to jump into Plymouth Sound from a Hercules.

she was going to be very frightened, but was determined to face the challenge. Having done so, and succeeded, it probably changed her life in that she must have then realised that she could now face up to any difficult task, however daunting.

When jumping at low level a 'static line' is used which is attached to the aircraft and this automatically opens the parachute as you jump out. It all happens very quickly and before you have time to think about it you are floating down in blissful silence and can thoroughly enjoy the sensation. I could see the Royal Marine boats below waiting to pick us up and, once we entered the water, within seconds we had been dragged into a boat by a burly Marine. On dry land I was met by our local ITV team who asked me for my reaction and, still being on cloud nine, I just said "bloody marvellous". I subsequently suffered a bit of stick from friends for my bad language, but it could have been much worse.

Also at Mount Batten was No. 3 (County of Devon) Maritime Headquarters Unit of the Royal Auxiliary Air Force. This was the first time I had come into close contact with the R Aux AF. Most of the members were in full-time civilian employment and I was most impressed with the way they gave, with great enthusiasm and dedication, so much of their so-called spare time to week-end training and exercises. They were fully supported, I must emphasise, by their friends and families. Their wartime role was to support the staffs in the Operations Rooms of the various Maritime Headquarters. Little did I realise that, some years later, I would be invited to become their Honorary Air Commodore. I still proudly wear the small 'A' on the lapels of my uniform to this day.

Our responsibility for the operation of the Search and Rescue organisation in the southern half of the UK, and also offshore, gave me the chance to visit our various SAR Helicopter Flights, the nearest one being at Chivenor on the north Devon coast. Also at Mount Batten was the RAF School of Combat Survival and Rescue where aircrew, inter alia, learn how to cope with landing in the sea after ejecting from their aircraft. The SAR helicopters would co-operate with the School by winching up the course students who had already spent several hours in a dinghy having been dumped overboard from one of the marine craft. This was good value for the students and it also gave the helicopter aircrews good winching practice, an exercise which requires very precise flying by the pilot and much skill and courage by the winch men in the back. The helicopters used to refuel on the lawn outside the front door of my Headquarters and I could walk the few yards from my office direct to the Whirlwind to do some winching, a most agreeable occupation.

I had watched and taken part in many practice rescues, but it was not until a quarter of a century later that, when Katharine and I were enjoying a Baltic cruise with SAGA (Send All Grannies Away), that we were able to witness a live helicopter casualty evacuation for the first time. We were having breakfast on deck at the beginning of our last day at sea when we saw a Sea King helicopter of the Royal Danish Navy arrive which then hovered over the upper deck. The captain announced that one of our elderly passengers had been taken ill during the night and the ship's doctor was not prepared to risk looking after him for a further 24 hours before we arrived back at Dover. The captain had therefore radioed for a helicopter to take the patient to the nearest hospital which was in Denmark some 80 miles away. It was all very exciting for the passengers to watch the patient, together with his wife and their luggage, being winched up into the helicopter yards away and we were relieved, later in the day, to hear that the patient had recovered satisfactorily.

One of the SAR helicopter flights was at Manston in Kent where the station also operated Chipmunks to give air experience to ATC cadets, and it was there, on 24th April 1980, that I flew my last solo flight with the RAF in one of these aircraft. It was an emotional experience to realise that I would probably never fly solo again and I cast my mind back to my first solo thirty-six years earlier; but nothing could, or was ever likely to eclipse that first event – or so I thought at the time.

My last flight in the RAF as a serving officer took place five days later when I carried out thirty minutes winching from Mount Batten. As I climbed out of the aircraft the crew presented me with a print of a Whirlwind, signed on the back by all the members of the aircrew who had flown with me in the aircraft and also the groundcrew who had prepared the Whirlwind for flight. What was so remarkable was that the print was a picture of the actual aircraft that I had just flown. That picture of XD186 is now one of my most treasured possessions.

Whirlwind XD186 in which I carried out my last flight as a serving officer. © John G Norriss

I retired from the RAF on my 55th birthday in August 1980, but as I was entitled to some leave and also some resettlement courses before I left the Service, I departed from Mount Batten three months earlier. Just before I left, and in accordance with tradition, I was 'dined out' at a Guest Night in the Officers' Mess. My Senior Air Staff Officer, Group Captain Iain Balderstone who was an old friend, made a very generous farewell speech and, in reply, I remember saying how much I was looking forward to retirement. As I sat down I realised it must have sounded as if I couldn't wait to get away from the place and that I did not enjoy my work. Nothing could have been further from the truth; all I meant was that there were many things I wanted to do, but that I had never had the time to follow them up while I was working. I also took the opportunity to publicly thank Katharine, who was present at the dinner, for being such a fantastic camp follower for the past twenty nine years during which time she had always given 100 per cent support to the service, often under difficult circumstances. She did, however, have the advantage of being brought up in a service environment with a father who had been a captain in the Royal Navy and both grandfathers who were generals, so she must have had some idea of what she was letting herself in for when she married me.

Mount Batten finally closed as an RAF station in 1992 when the land and buildings were handed over to the Plymouth Development Corporation. They were then responsible for today's modern facilities which include a yachting marina. Prior to the closure, the roles of SOUMAR and NORMAR had been taken over by HQ 18 Group at Northwood.

* * *

We had bought our first house, a cottage in Somerset, two years before I retired. I spent the first few months after I left Mount Batten generally unwinding and doing lots of DIY on the house. I also did two very useful resettlement courses. The first was a House Maintenance Course with the Army at Aldershot. This is a first-class course where everyone wears overalls with no ranks visible so that generals and privates can muck in together in a very relaxed atmosphere. I came away realizing that amateurs could do as good a job as most professionals at basic redecoration, and even some more serious structural work, but, as I was to find out, the amateurs take three times as long to do the job.

The second course was a six-week Business Management Appreciation course with the London Polytechnic. This course is obviously far too short to be able to give one any sort of qualifications, but it did give the students an introduction to business attitudes, financial implications and even Trade Union considerations etc. The course was led by a retired Ghurka Colonel who had led a successful business career after he left the Army. He was pleased when I told him that I seriously intended to get a job to top up my pension because he said it was astonishing how many senior officers had died soon after their retirement having gone down 'leafy lane'. It seems that if one has led a very active life and then suddenly slows down, with one's feet up watching sport on the TV or whatever, that the body itself sometimes just gives up.

Soon after I had completed my two resettlement courses I was asked by MOD to do a study into the career structure of the Air Traffic and Fighter Control officers in the RAF General Duties Ground Branch. This was to be a four month-contract as a Civil Servant, paid as if in the grade of Assistant Secretary. I was getting nowhere fast in trying to get a job so I gladly accepted the invitation.

The first thing I did was to see what had happened to some of the similar studies in the past. I soon found out that there was considerable scepticism amongst those who were the subject of the studies because they did not think much had been achieved in concrete terms. I suspected that one of the reasons may have been because the chairman might have submitted his findings to the Air Force Board without first testing the recommendations with those staffs who would be asked to implement them. I therefore determined to work closely with the relevant staffs so that I could be confident that they would support my recommendations for Air Force Board approval.

There were many problems with the GD Ground Branch at that time. The basic difficulty was that the shape of the 'career pyramid' was far too flat in that there were very few senior posts with a very large number of junior officers (mostly flight lieutenants) with little chance of promotion and no compensating pay increments for long service. Morale was, understandably, low. I have always thought that the most important factor in solving problems was to make sure that you really understood what the problem was in the first place. Over the next few months, together with my team of two Air Traffic Control officers and one Fighter Controller, I interviewed in groups about half the members of the entire Branch throughout the RAF, both at home and overseas, to find out what they thought the problems were. A pattern of recommendations began to emerge, but some would be so expensive that there was no chance of them being approved. Therefore, in consultation with the staffs, we set about making some compromises and it was very gratifying that we achieved some measure of success.

At that time none of the Air Traffic Control girls in the WRAF had ever been promoted beyond flight lieutenant. They believed that there was no prospect of promotion to squadron leader because it was prohibited as a matter of policy. I had great difficulty in explaining that there was no such policy and that they really were considered solely on merit, and that the reason why none of them had been promoted was because those good enough to be considered, thinking that there was no chance of going forward, had decided to leave the Service. I told them that if they stayed in the RAF they would be considered on equal terms with their male colleagues. Soon after I had completed my study I was delighted to see that some of them had been promoted just as I forecasted. Not all my recommendations were accepted, but many were and it was very rewarding subsequently to receive a number of messages of appreciation from those who had benefited.

My report was to be produced on a word processor. I had never seen one of these newfangled devices and it is hard to believe that in 1980 they were an innovation. It is inconceivable now that any office could be run without one. Even copying machines had only recently become commonplace. I remember in the 1960s that if I wanted to have something copied, my poor unfortunate clerk had to type it all out.

Shortly before I completed my study, which became known as the Severne Report, I received a telephone call from the Personal Staff Officer to the Air Member for Personnel (AMP), Air Marshal Charles Ness, whom I had known when he was station commander at Steamer Point in Aden. AMP wanted to see me 'next Thursday'. I was of course retired from the RAF and I couldn't imagine why he could possibly want to see me because I was reasonably confident that I hadn't done anything seriously wrong. It just so happened that it was not convenient for me to go up to London on that day and I didn't particularly want to go and see AMP in any case. The PSO on the other end of the telephone was getting more and more embarrassed as this conversation continued and he then said: 'But AMP is coming in from leave especially to see you.' At this point I gave way. When I met Charles Ness in his office the following week he just said, 'The Queen would like you to become Captain of The Queen's Flight.' I said, 'Is that a command or is it an invitation?' To which he replied, 'It is an invitation – you have forty-eight hours to make up your mind.'

Chapter 17
The Queen's Flight

The title 'Captain of The Queen's Flight' can be traced back to the *London Gazette* of 20th July 1936 which stated, inter alia:

> The King has been graciously pleased to make the following appointment to His Majesty's Household, to date from the 21st July 1936: Flight Lieutenant Edward Hedley Fielden, AFC, Captain of The King's Flight.

When the Prince of Wales became King Edward VIII in 1936 the Air Ministry agreed to form The King's Flight which at that time consisted of one aircraft, a pilot, a secretary and two engineers. 'Mouse' Fielden, as he was known to all his friends, was the pilot of the one and only aircraft of The King's Flight, and therefore the title 'Captain' accurately described his role. He was supported by two civilian engineers with NCO status and a civilian secretary. The aircraft was the King's privately owned De Havilland Rapide, G-ADDD. The first aircraft to be publicly financed was the Airspeed Envoy, G-AEXX, which was delivered in May 1937. Incidentally, Neville Shute, an aeronautical engineer, was the founder of Airspeed Ltd in 1931.

Edward Fielden in his pre-war full dress uniform of the RAF. The Queen's Flight Association

Edward VIII arriving at Mildenhall in 1936 for the Royal Review in the first aircraft used by the King's Flight. The Queen's Flight Association

The Airspeed Envoy, the first publicly funded aircraft of The King's Flight. The Queen's Flight Association

The first member of the Royal Family to fly was the Prince of Wales who, in 1917, was taken up in an RE8 close to the Western Front in France. He flew again just after the War with Major Barker VC who was still recovering from wounds and piloted the aircraft with one arm in a sling. When George V heard about this he was not amused and advised his sons not to fly again, however Prince Albert, later George VI, became the first member of the Royal Family to gain his RAF wings after a course in 1919 flying Avro 504s.

It took some years for George V's attitude to change and it was not until 1928 that that the Prince of Wales again took up flying. After several flights with the RAF he bought his own aircraft, a De Havilland Gipsy Moth, G-AALG, which he had finished in the red and blue colours of the Brigade of Guards and which has been the colour scheme that has been used ever since in various forms for all royal aircraft. 'Mouse' Fielden, then a serving flight lieutenant, was appointed as his personal pilot and he looked after the Prince's aircraft, initially at Northolt and subsequently at Hendon. Over the next few years the Prince of Wales bought a series of light aircraft culminating in the Rapide G-ADDD. When King George V died at Sandringham in 1936 The Prince became Edward VIII. The new King had to attend the Accession Council in London the next day and Mouse Fielden flew him down to Hendon from Bircham Newton in the Rapide. Since George V had never flown, this was the first occasion that a British Monarch had taken to the air.

To celebrate King George V's Silver Jubilee in 1935 a Royal Review of the Royal Air Force was held at Mildenhall. Before departing for the airfield, Vandyk took a photograph in the garden of Buckingham Palace of the King, accompanied by his two sons, the Prince of Wales – later to become Edward VIII – and the Duke of York – later to become George VI. When I was researching the history of royal flying in the Royal Archives – which incidentally are held in the Round Tower at Windsor castle – the archivist produced the famous original picture of the 'Three Kings', the only photograph ever taken of them together in RAF uniform. To my delight it was signed, whereas none of the copies seen elsewhere had the royal signatures. It is a well known photograph and copies are to be seen hung in the corridors of many RAF Officers' and Sergeants' Messes. The Queen subsequently gave permission for copies of the original to be made available to members of The Queen's Flight.

The King's Flight was disbanded during the Second World War and in 1942 it was absorbed into No. 161 Squadron at Newmarket. This squadron carried out special duties operations, initially with Wing Commander Fielden as the new squadron commander. The squadron then moved to Tempsford with Group Captain Fielden as the station commander. Throughout the War Mouse

The 'Three Kings' photographed on the occasion of the Royal Review at Mildenhall in 1935. The Royal Archives

Fielden retained his title of 'Captain of the King's Flight' and was responsible for organizing any flying the King or other members of the Royal Family might wish to carry out.

The King's Flight was reformed in 1946 at RAF Benson with four Vickers Vikings. Fielden was by now an Air Commodore. The first major commitment of the post-war Flight was to take part in the Royal Tour of South Africa in 1947. The Royal Family sailed to Cape Town and used the Vikings for flying within South Africa and Rhodesia, now Zimbabwe. The monarch and the heir to the throne never flew together so the King and Princess Margaret flew in one aircraft, the Queen and Princess Elizabeth in the second and the ground crew and spares in the third. It was during this tour that our present Queen flew for the first time and on the 21st April 1947, at Government House Cape Town, on the occasion of the 21st birthday of Princess Elizabeth, Air Commodore Fielden presented HRH with a diamond wings brooch on behalf of all members of The King's Flight. On the same day the Princess made that historic broadcast to the Commonwealth in which she said, 'I declare before you all that my whole life, whether it be long or short, shall be devoted to your service.'

When I first became involved in 1958 as The Duke of Edinburgh's Equerry, the Flight consisted of three De Havilland Herons, one of which was for Prince Philip's personal use, two Westland Whirlwind helicopters and a De Havilland Dove. The Dove had been allocated to the Flight in 1953 for HRH's flying instruction and was subsequently used for some of his official visits.

On 1st January 1962 Mouse Fielden retired from The Queen's Flight as an Air Vice-Marshal and was appointed Senior Air Equerry to the Queen. He had joined the RAF in 1924, became personal pilot to the Prince of Wales in 1929 as a flight lieutenant, founded The King's Flight in 1936 and subsequently held an unbroken connection with the Royal family for forty years. He cherished highly the honour that he had been decorated by four British monarchs: AFC from George V, MVO from Edward VIII, DFC, CB and CVO from George V and KCVO and GCVO from Elizabeth II. What a remarkable record.

I succeeded Archie Winskill as Captain of The Queen's Flight in 1982 with half a day's handover. I remember asking him what happened if an engine didn't start at the beginning of a royal flight. He just said: 'It wouldn't dare!' End of story.

We had five aircraft and about 200 personnel, very different to the original King's Flight of 1936. There was now a wing commander who was the commanding officer of the Flight and he was also the Queen's pilot. My role, in addition to having overall responsibility for the Flight, was to give advice to the Queen and members of the Royal Family on all aspects of aviation. This might involve anything from organising the air travel arrangements for a State Visit overseas by the Queen, arranging a parachute jump for a young prince or the supervision of the flying training of a young duchess. The work was thus very varied and required a good practical knowledge of all aspects of aviation. Although I did not fly The Queen's Flight aircraft with members of the royal family on board, I still retained the historic title. The Captain of The Queen's Flight was a member of the Royal Household, as was the Flag Officer Royal Yachts, the captain of HMY *Britannia*.

We had three Hawker Siddeley Andovers which entered service with The Queen's Flight in 1964. I had never flown an Andover, but I wanted to be able to land the aircraft safely in the very unlikely event of both pilots becoming incapacitated for any reason – at least that was my excuse to have some dual instruction on the aircraft soon after I arrived.

We also had two Westland Wessex Helicopters which arrived in 1969 and I frequently flew these aircraft home after a royal flight. We operated them with a navigator and he would vacate his seat for me on the return flight home. In the case of the Andover, if I took the place of a co-pilot I would be depriving him of much needed practice because he was not allowed to fly the aircraft when the royal passengers were on board. I therefore confined all my flying to the Wessex which was fine by me.

Since we occasionally flew over the sea I thought all the helicopter crews and I should carry out the 'Underwater Escape Training' held at HMS *Heron* at Yeovilton. My reasoning was that we should do all we could to know how best to help our royal passengers escape if we should be forced to ditch. Commonly called 'The Dunker', the victims are taught how best to escape from a simulated cabin of a Lynx helicopter which is submerged in a swimming pool, in the dark, and then turned upside down. I am a keen swimmer and I enjoyed the experience, but it must be extremely daunting for those not so fond of the water. It was reassuring to see that we were monitored by lifeguards who could pull us out if we got into trouble. It is certainly a very valuable training aid.

Our passengers were all those members of the Royal Family who carried out public duties, the Chiefs of the three services and Government ministers, together with the foreign equivalents when they visited this country. I always escorted the Queen and the Queen Mother as 'Commodore' whenever they flew anywhere in the world, whether or not they were in one of our aircraft. By the time I retired in 1989 I had flown with the Queen 256 times and the Queen Mother, 195. I had two deputies, both group captains, one of whom was also the station commander at RAF Benson. Between the three of us we would liaise with the various royal households to plan foreign tours and then escort our royal passengers whenever they took to the air. My two deputies normally flew as 'Commodore' with the other members of the Royal Family, but I would take their place if they were otherwise committed. I might have expected The Captain of The Queen's Flight and his two deputies to be experienced transport operators, but in fact all three of us were ex-Lightning pilots.

Way back in 1959 I had seen the useful role played by the 'Commodore' when 'Mouse' Fielden flew with the Duke of Edinburgh on the Royal Tour to India and Pakistan in the BOAC Comet. Prince Philip had just one person with whom he could discuss the flying arrangements, which of course included all the protocol aspects of arrivals and departures and any changes to the programme, without having to bother the captain of the aircraft who had his

A young Prince William thanks Group Captain Jeremy Jones, Deputy Captain, after a flight.
The Queen's Flight Association

own problems to look after. In turn, the aircraft captain only had one person to talk to on behalf of all the passengers. Whenever the Duke of Edinburgh or the Prince of Wales flew they usually piloted the aircraft themselves. Each had their own qualified flying instructor appointed who was captain of the aircraft.

The Duke of Edinburgh gained his RAF wings in 1953 having been taught by Caryl Gordon who had led the CFS Meteor Aerobatic Team back in the fifties. HRH had qualified as a helicopter pilot with the Royal Navy in 1956 and was awarded his private pilot's licence in 1959. He flew 5,986 hours in 59 types of aircraft. He was very fit and always had a most professional approach to flying. I therefore had no qualms about his flying beyond the normal retirement age for airline or RAF pilots. Prince Philip's final flight at the age of 76 was on 11th August 1997 from Carlisle to Islay. A fortnight before that he had hosted a splendid 'Captains, Pilots and Navigator's Dinner' at Frogmore House, Windsor. All those members of The Queen's Flight who had been associated with his flying were invited and, as the senior member of that august body, I found myself making the speech of thanks. This I have reproduced in full because it illustrates HRH's genuine life-long interest in flying:

'Each one of us was thrilled to be invited to this unique occasion and it fell upon me to express our thanks to His Royal Highness and to say how grateful we all are to be here.

I am reminded of the Christian who was thrown to the lions, but who managed to walk away unscathed. When asked how he managed it he said: "Oh, I just whispered in his ear that it was the custom after a good meal to make a speech". So the lion thought better of it.

I know Your Royal Highness's interest in aviation goes back to your days at Kurt Hahn's school at Salem in 1933 when, with an American boy, you decided to design and build a biplane glider, one which today would be called a hang glider and, from the sound of it, one which was well ahead of its time. You had finished the airframe, but before you had time to cover the wings with fabric, the Nazis intervened. I have a feeling that the Nazis did us a good turn because it was your intention to launch yourself off the top of a hill.

At Gordonstoun, just before the War, your interest in aviation was such that your first inclination was to join the RAF, but you had reckoned without the influence of your uncle who was, as you put it, "a more than normally enthusiastic naval officer".

However, after the late King died, you found yourself wearing RAF uniform for the first time, *starting* with the rank of Marshal of the Royal Air Force, and this gave you the opportunity to gain your wings with the RAF on fixed-wing aircraft. Since you were also an Admiral of the Fleet, you subsequently qualified as a helicopter pilot with the Royal Navy. All this was a long time ago and during the intervening years you have continued to impress us all with your enthusiasm for flying and, above all, with your thoroughly professional approach to it.

Your encouragement and support of private and sporting flying, through your involvement as President of the Royal Aero Club, and as an honorary member of the Tiger Club, gave a much needed shot in the arm to the movement during the 60s, particularly with your initiative for Formula One Air Racing and the Dawn-to-Dusk competition. During this time you became the only member of the Royal Family ever to have flown a single seat aircraft, even if you were nearly scalped in the process.

The aircraft industry as a whole has benefitted from your interest and encouragement; this is well illustrated by the number of proto-types you have managed to fly, much to the envy of many of us.

We recognise that, more than anyone else, you have had a considerable influence on the way royal flying has evolved in the post Mouse Fielden era, not only with the choice of aircraft for The Queen's Flight, but by blazing a trail round the world to some unlikely places, and demonstrating how the Royal Family can make the best use of aviation, despite all sorts of difficulties put in your way by ministers and air marshals. The special relationship you generate with your crews is well known and greatly valued by them.

Many pilots lose the urge to continue flying as the years creep on, but to the delight of us all, you have retained your enthusiasm and determination to remain in good flying practice up to the present time – and now we understand you have decided to leave the flight deck and let some of the others do the driving. 32 Squadron will undoubtedly miss you up the front end, but your crews will, of course, continue to enjoy flying with you for many years to come.

Sir, it has been a tremendous privilege for us all to have flown with you whether as pilot, navigator, crew member, or like myself as a mere passenger, and I end as I began by thanking Your Royal Highness for inviting us to be part of this unique and thoroughly enjoyable occasion'.

The Andovers were excellent aircraft and did a good job, but they were getting a bit old and were not ideal for long distance flying because they were relatively slow and, unlike a jet, could not climb above seriously bad weather. Moreover I thought the Queen must be just about the only head of state in the world still flying around in a propeller driven aircraft. We therefore considered the ideal aircraft for the Andover's replacement. I thought such an airliner should be British, failing that one built in the Commonwealth or at least one with major British components such as the engines. We looked at a number of aircraft, but it just so happened that the new British Aerospace 146 was ideal for our requirements, and it was available. Furthermore the Prime Minister,

Michael Turner's painting of a Queen's Flight Andover over Windsor Castle. Michael Turner

Margaret Thatcher, was keen to see it selling well overseas – what better advertisement could there be than for the Queen to be seen flying round the world in this new British aircraft? To our delight two aircraft were then ordered and the first one was handed over to me by the Chairman of British

Robert Taylor's painting presented by British Aerospace on the occasion of the handing over of the first BAe 146 to the Queen's Flight. Queen's Flight by Robert Taylor – © The Military Gallery, Wendover, England

Aerospace, Sir Austin Pearce, at a ceremony at Hatfield in April 1986, our fiftieth anniversary year. At the same time he presented us with a superb painting by Robert Taylor, one which depicted the new BAe 146 flying over the current Andover and Wessex and also the Rapide G-ADDD, the first aircraft of the original King's Flight. The 146 was tailor-made for our role in that it was about the right size and had the best short-field performance of any jet airliner in the world. We could operate out of short 1,000-yard strips and this was to come in very useful when flying in Third World countries.

My father had always used '777' on the number plates of his cars in the 1930s and so, back in 1959, I thought I would continue the tradition by giving my wife the number 'KV7' for a wedding anniversary present. I have since read that she is the only person with her name, Katherine Veronica Severne, on a number plate. We found it on a Coventry scrap dump and the dealer did not want anything for it – the craze for personalized number plates had not yet started and they had no financial value at that time. We still have the number plate and things are very different now. With all this in mind I thought it would be fun to have our 146s with '700' in the number, not because of my name, but because the Form 700 is the one used for preparing an aircraft for flight and is very well known by all those in the RAF who are involved with aircraft. I was pleased that the first aircraft handed over was ZE700, followed by 701; 702 was reserved for the third 146.

To celebrate our fiftieth anniversary in 1986 we produced a book *'The Queen's Flight – Fifty years of Royal Flying'*. We also held a reception in St James's Palace which was attended by the Queen, the Duke of Edinburgh, the

'50 Years Apart'. The Rapide restored in the original colours of the King's Flight of 1936 and the first BAe 146 of 1986.

The Families' Day on the Fiftieth Birthday of the Queen's Flight with the new 146, celebrated with the Turbulent flown by the Duke of Edinburgh and a half scale model. Michael Jones

Prince and Princess of Wales, Princess Margaret, Prince Edward, Princess Alice, the Duke and Duchess of Gloucester and the Duke and Duchess of Kent. The reception was attended by all members of the Flight and during the evening I presented Her Majesty with a specially bound copy of the book which was hot off the press. It was indeed a memorable occasion.

We also held a 'Families Day' on 26th July which was very close to the founding day of 20th July fifty years earlier. In addition to several visiting aircraft associated with royal flying, we had the Turbulent which had been flown by the Duke of Edinburgh and had been entered by him in the 1960 King's Cup Air Race, together with a splendid half-scale radio-controlled model, both of which were photographed against our new 146.

Soon after I arrived I decided to set up a Queen's Flight Museum. There was a great deal of interesting information concerning royal flying in general and I thought it was important to have this recorded while there were still people around who could remember and contribute. I knew Mouse Fielden well and his widow was most helpful in donating a uniform, log books and various memorabilia. I also obtained, on loan from the RAF Museum at Hendon, some superb models of the early King's Flight aircraft and some of those personally owned by the then Prince of Wales in the 1930s. The Museum was opened by the Duchess of Gloucester in 1987. After The Queen's Flight disbanded in 1995 the contents of the Museum were taken over by 32 Squadron at Northolt which maintains to this day an excellent 'Museum of Royal Flying'.

The BBC wanted to make a documentary about The Queen's Flight and fifty years of royal flying. I was happy for them to do this provided I could check the script for accuracy and any matters which might affect our security. Over the years bitter experiences have made me somewhat sceptical concerning the ability of the media in general and the BBC in particular to portray their subjects accurately. They refused what I thought was a reasonable request, consequently I did not allow them the facilities they needed to make the film. The Reader's Digest, on the other hand, took a completely different view. One of their editors called on me to ask if they could write an article to celebrate our fiftieth birthday. I made the same condition that I put to the BBC and received the following reply, 'Of course, we value our reputation far too much for us not to agree to your request.' In the event, they wrote a very good article and I only had to make one small correction on a point of fact.

When the Queen carried out State Visits overseas the aircraft of The Queen's Flight were not big enough to carry the required load of up to fifty passengers and about eight tons of baggage. Neither did they have the range if the Queen was to avoid several refuelling stops on the way, say, to the Far East. Such stops would normally involve the usual arrival formalities. Her Majesty therefore would either fly in a VC10 of the RAF or charter an airliner from British Airways. If flying to Canada or Australia those countries would provide the aircraft, at that time military 707s. The Queen never flew in foreign aircraft except in the United States so, if internal flying was required in the country being visited, a Queen's Flight aircraft would be pre-positioned.

Prior to a State visit, one of the Queen's Private Secretaries would lead a team to carry out a reconnaissance visit to plan the tour which might typically last a fortnight or so. A draft would have been produced by our Ambassador and recommended by the Foreign and Commonwealth office. The team normally included The Queen's Personal Protection Officer to consider security matters, the 'Medical Officer to The Queen Abroad' to cover possible medical emergencies, the Buckingham Palace 'Sergeant Footman' who looks after all the luggage arrangements, one of the Private Secretary's lady clerks and me. Once in the country to be visited we would normally be joined by our ambassador. We would then go over the whole proposed programme and consider alternatives. On these recces, as we called them, the Royal Household team would often use a Queen's Flight aircraft because much time could be saved by not having to book infrequent internal flights, if they existed at all. They also gave valuable experience to the crews as proving flights. On our return the Private Secretary would make his recommendations to Her Majesty for her approval.

In 1983 the Queen and the Duke of Edinburgh carried out a major tour to the Caribbean, Mexico, The United States and Canada. We flew out in a VC10 and most of the flying, once we arrived in USA, was in the famous Boeing 707

'Special Air Mission 26000'. Although this aircraft was popularly known as 'Air Force One', that is actually the call sign which is used whenever the President is flying, regardless of the aircraft type. 26000 was the first jet presidential aircraft and became famous when it flew President Kennedy to Berlin where he made his 'Ich bin ein Berliner' speech and again the following year when it carried his body to Washington after his assassination. The 707 was delivered to Andrew's Air Force Base at Washington in 1962 and cost $8m. Thirty-six years later this famous aircraft was retired to Dayton, Ohio, to join other historic presidential planes at Wright-Patterson Field.

On arrival at Long Beach, California, I had been booked into the Queen Mary Hotel. In my naivety I imagined a comfortable hotel of the 1920s or 1930s – in fact, of course it was RMS *Queen Mary*, the liner which had been cleverly converted and was permanently moored in a basin. I had not realized how big it was until I actually saw it. Close by was the museum which housed Howard Hughes' huge HK-1 Hercules, the flying boat with a wingspan of 320 ft, the largest span of any aircraft ever built. It was designed in 1942 and built of wood, because the government said it must not be constructed from materials critical to the war effort, such as steel or aluminium, hence its nickname of 'The Spruce Goose'. It was intended to be capable of ferrying 750 troops across the Atlantic, but many difficulties were encountered during its construction. It was not finished until 1947 when Howard Hughes unexpectedly flew the aircraft for about a mile at an altitude of 70 ft. It never flew again. I was greatly looking forward to seeing this splendid 8 engined-giant, but unfortunately the museum was not due open until later in the year. The HK-1 was finally acquired in 1993 by the Evergreen International Aviation Museum in McMinnville, Oregon.

While I was staying in The *Queen Mary*, the Queen and the President were staying in the Royal Yacht moored close by. There was a terrific storm that night and the weather was so bad the following morning that it was decided not to sail up to San Francisco, but to fly there instead. The floods on the route to the airport were too deep for the cars so the Queen and the royal party drove to the airport in a US Navy coach. I met the Queen at the airfield and tried to shelter her with an umbrella for the short walk to the aircraft, but the umbrella promptly blew inside out. In the press the next day there was a marvellous picture of the Queen under the broken brolly roaring with laughter, but unfortunately I never kept a copy. It was a memorable visit, there was even a minor earth tremor to add excitement to the occasion.

One of the most interesting State Visits was the one to China in 1986. Not only was this the fiftieth year of royal flying with the King's Flight and The Queen's Flight, but it was to be the first time a British monarch had ever visited China.

Foreign aircraft flying over China are required to keep to the international airways where English is universally used by pilots and air traffic controllers. If there is a requirement to fly outside these controlled airspaces, as we wished to do, we had to carry a Chinese radio officer to interpret. The recce in our 146, which was flown by the CO of the Flight, the Queen's pilot, was interesting because it was sometimes difficult to get accurate answers from our Chinese interpreter. Perhaps because of the innate courtesy of the Chinese he gave us the impression that he felt he ought to give us the answers we wanted to hear which were not necessarily the correct ones. When trying to check on airfield facilities, and so on, this could be tricky. The Chinese radio operator would not allow us to see the route charts with details of the facilities of all the airfields, military and civil, which we might wish to use in case we needed to divert in an emergency, but luckily I managed to 'borrow' one of his charts for a few minutes during the flight and I made a photo copy using the copier we had on board. I was rather pleased with myself and went forward to the pilot to tell him what I had done. 'I've been there already' he said. We do our best.

We chartered a Tristar from British Airways, one of the aircraft which was subsequently bought by the RAF, and flew to Peking, or Beijing as it is now called, with one re-fuelling stop in Oman. Once in China most of the internal flying was to be carried out by our 146. This was only the second royal tour using our new aircraft and all eyes were on it because the Chinese Government were considering buying some. An unserviceable aircraft would have been politically disastrous.

From my point of view it was a most memorable and enjoyable tour because, amongst other attractions, we visited the Great Wall and the Terracotta Warriors, two of the world's most famous tourist venues. I was very impressed by the talent I witnessed at the schools and I thought that if they could only solve their population problem, China would become a leading industrial power. In fact the advances made in the last few years have confirmed those first impressions.

On 6th August 1985, to celebrate the Queen Mother's 85th birthday two days earlier, British Airways organised a flight in Concorde G–BOAF for Her Majesty. The other passengers were representatives of every department of the airline. During the two hour flight we went supersonic and the Queen Mother chatted to all the passengers and also visited the flight deck. This was my only flight in that magnificent aircraft and I couldn't help thinking at the time that we were cruising higher and faster than any of those fighters I used to fly in the past.

When heads of state visited Britain on a formal visit they would normally travel outside London to at least one venue and, if travelling by air, I would accompany them in one of our aircraft. When I flew with Sultan Qaboos of Oman to watch a firepower demonstration, someone pointed out to me that he

Sultan Qaboos of Oman landed at Bovington for a firepower demonstration in 1982. He was greeted by the Lord Lieutenant of Dorset. The Queen's Flight Association

was wearing a smart new army great coat which had been made in London specially for the visit – apparently his badges of rank on his shoulders were made of solid gold.

When the Queen Mother visited Oslo in 1983 for the 80th birthday of King Olav V, I sat next to a Norwegian diplomat at the state dinner and asked him if there was any suggestion of a republican movement in the country. He replied, 'Yes, but it never gets anywhere because everyone would vote for President Olav.' He was extremely popular and was known as the People's King. In his younger days he had not only jumped off the Holmenkollen Ski Jump in Oslo, but won a gold medal for sailing at the Summer Olympics in Amsterdam in 1928.

On another occasion we were due to visit Kent by helicopter with the Queen Mother when, shortly after taking off from her home at Royal Lodge in Windsor Great Park, one of the two engines decided to quit. While the Wessex can fly well on one engine, the safety factor is obviously reduced and the pilot therefore decided to do a precautionary landing on the polo ground in the Park. We were amazed to be met by several press photographers who had been hoping to snatch a photograph of the Queen out riding with President Reagan who was visiting Britain on a state visit. On meeting the gentlemen of the Press

Her Majesty just said, 'The wretched thing has broken down!' Meanwhile, The Queen's Flight machine went into overdrive and in a remarkably short space of time an Andover was positioned at Heathrow for the visit to be carried out by fixed wing and car.

All members of The Queen's Flight were volunteers. The majority of our 180 airmen were engineers and they had either volunteered for the job or had been selected for interview. They would all spend the morning with their peers seeing what the job involved and then they would be interviewed in the afternoon. At that point they were asked if they wanted to join the Flight. A few were put off by the extremely high standards they witnessed, particularly the spotless hangar floor, and by the warning that weekends could be cancelled at short notice if they were required to work on an unserviceable aircraft. Anyone involved with aeroplanes knows about their tendency to go u/s on a Friday afternoon. In this case we would work on the aircraft until it was serviceable, even if it was not scheduled to fly, just in case an emergency turned up. Those candidates who then agreed to join the Flight had, in my book, become volunteers. The spirit on 'the hangar floor' was remarkable and I was proud to be associated with such a professional and enthusiastic body.

The serviceability rate was very impressive and it was indeed rare for an aircraft not to be able to take off on time. Arrival times were based on 'doors open' rather than landing times, because that was when the programme for a royal visit begins. The crews were very skilled at stopping opposite the red carpet – if there was one – and opening the door within 5 seconds of the scheduled time. One gained the impression that nothing ever went wrong and that everything always worked like clockwork, but of course problems did arise and I soon found out that the CO and the whole team were adept at managing a crisis quickly and effectively without telling me or seeking help from 'higher authority'. In fact I am sure that it was probably a good thing that I did not know about some of the problems and the way they were solved.

In 1988 I had a good demonstration of the sort of dilemmas the Flight had to deal with. I had planned to escort the Prince and Princess of Wales from Paris to Lyneham on the afternoon of Friday 11th November after their State Visit. This was to be my last flight with Their Royal Highnesses before I retired and I was particularly anxious that everything should run like the usual clockwork.

There were too many staff and too much baggage to fit into one aircraft together with the royal party. Since we did not have a second aircraft available we therefore planned to fly the staff and baggage from Paris in the morning; I would then meet the aircraft at Northolt and return to Paris to fetch TRHs in the afternoon.

It all started to go wrong the day before when our Air Attaché rang me from Paris to say that the French Air Traffic Controllers had just gone on strike and although they were prepared to let the royal flight depart on time the next day, they would not guarantee the departure for the staff flight in the morning, or even agree to let it return to fetch the Prince and Princess in the afternoon. I had a problem: if I cancelled the staff flight in order to guarantee the availability of an aircraft for the Royal Flight, TRHs would arrive home with no staff or baggage and I would end up in the Tower. On the other hand if I let the staff flight go in the morning and the aircraft could not return to fetch TRHs, I would end up in the Tower, without my head. One thing I had learnt during my time with The Queen's Flight was the incredible resourcefulness of all its members and I was confident that they would somehow find a solution to these frustrating problems. I therefore decided to stick to the original plan. No sooner had I made this decision than I was told that the French now insisted that the staff flight be brought forward by two hours. This meant a very early start for the staff, but in the event they coped magnificently.

By now I was beginning to think some rather uncharitable things about the French Air Traffic Controllers when, early on the Friday morning, I was told that the British Air Traffic Control computer had broken down which meant that our staff flight in the morning would not be allowed into Northolt. After a lot of fast talking by Graham Laurie, the captain of our 146, the staff flight was allowed in although its take-off was delayed by thirty minutes. I therefore set off from Benson by car to join the aircraft at Northolt, a journey of about forty-five minutes.

Five miles from Northolt we ran into the next problem – fog – and I knew our 146 would not be able to land. This was in the days before mobile phones and, since I had no radio in the car, I had no option but to continue to Northolt to find out where our aircraft had been diverted to. I was met at the gate and told it had gone to Heathrow, so we set off to the usual VIP stand on the south side where we are always positioned for royal flights. Imagine my horror when I saw a large African aircraft sitting on 'our' stand with an important looking black gentleman inspecting his guard of honour. He turned out to be the President of Senegal returning home after a state visit to Britain. I was then told that our aircraft was at Terminal 4 where I eventually found some very relieved passengers and a cheerful Graham Laurie and his crew all ready to sort out the next impossible problem.

We soon found it. The British computer had just come back on line, but there was a three-hour log jam and this would make our arrival at Paris late for the royal flight home. After some more fast talking we were allowed to take off, but when we arrived at Paris, would you believe it – there was the Senegal aircraft sitting on 'our' stand. After it was removed we were then able to park in the exact position required for the formal farewell ceremonies. However, on getting out of our aircraft I found there was a large patch of oil which had been deposited by the leaking African aircraft, just where the Prince and Princess would be walking. This was rapidly cleared up before the red carpet was laid.

In the meantime Prince Charles had decided to return to Kemble which was closer to Highgrove that our intended destination of Lyneham. Apart from the difficulty of asking an American-run base to remain open after their normal closing hours, the weather forecast was awful, so I stuck my neck out and said we would keep to the original plan and go to Lyneham.

Just to add to all this confusion, the co-pilot had locked the imprest in the safe in his Paris hotel and could not unlock it (the imprest is a fairly large sum of local currency to pay for the crew hotel expenses and any charges that might be incurred by the aircraft). The only man who had the master code was the manager and no one knew how to contact him for three days because it was a public holiday. We tried to borrow from the hotel, but they only had 20Fr in the till.

The State Visit was apparently a great success and I am sure to this day that our royal passengers had absolutely no idea of the dramas which led to a smooth, pleasant and completely uneventful flight home.

Shortly before I retired I was invited to Buckingham Palace for an audience with the Queen. This would be the opportunity for me to take my leave of her Majesty and to express my gratitude for the privilege of being able to serve the Royal Family in such an exciting and rewarding capacity. I arrived in plenty of time for fear of being held up in traffic and took the opportunity to say farewell to those with whom I had been working during the past seven years. In one of the corridors I met Sir William Heseltine, the Queen's Private Secretary, who said, 'I feel I must warn you that when you enter the Audience Room you will be confronted by a fully armed monarch.' He was right – there was the Queen, sword in hand, who then conferred upon me the honour of Knighthood and invested me with the Insignia of a Knight Commander of the Royal Victorian Order (KCVO). Then followed a very pleasant ten minutes or so discussing the past few years. The first thing I did when I left the Audience Room was to ring Katharine to tell her that she was going to have to get used to a new handle.

Earlier in 1984 I had been appointed as an Extra Equerry to the Queen which meant I could remain a member of the Royal Household for the rest of my life.

On handing over the reins to Air Commodore the Hon Timothy Elworthy – another Lightning pilot – I retired for the second time at the beginning of 1989. The Queen's Flight was, in my opinion, a very efficient organisation with an excellent record and very high morale. Sadly, the Government decided to disband it in 1995 and Tim had the difficult task of organising a smooth handover of the aircraft to 32 (The Royal) Squadron at Northolt, and also of setting up a new organization in Buckingham Palace for the tasking of royal flying under a Director of Royal Travel, a serving group captain.

Captain of The Queen's Flight 1982–1989.

Until now the costs of flying Queen's Flight aircraft had been borne by the Ministry of Defence, but under the new organisation the costs of official royal travel by air is now met by the Royal Travel Grant-in-Aid, the annual funding provided by the Department for Transport. The cost of any unofficial flying is met by the relevant Royal Household.

The Wessex helicopters had been in service since 1969 and were expensive to maintain and operate. Since no new economical helicopter was offered by the RAF, Tim Elworthy arranged for a civil helicopter, a Sikorsky S76, to be based at Blackbushe and tasked and operated by The Royal Household. The aircraft is finished in the red and blue colours of the Brigade of Guards as were the original aircraft of The King's Flight in 1936. Back to square one.

* * *

Not long after I retired for the second time the Lord-Lieutenant of Somerset, Colonel Walter Luttrell, invited me to become one of his Deputy Lieutenants (DL). I was surprised at this because I was not a Somerset person, having lived in the County for only ten years or so, but I was assured that 'lengthy residence in the County is not a qualification'. My name was submitted to Buckingham Palace for approval and the Lord-Lieutenant received the delightfully archaic reply that 'Her Majesty does not disapprove of the nomination'.

The background to the role of both Lord-Lieutenant and Deputy Lieutenant is interesting. Her Majesty's Lord-Lieutenants are the representatives of the Crown for each County; they are appointed by the Queen on the advice of the Prime Minister and were originally appointed by Henry VIII in the 1540s to take over the military duties of the Sheriff and to control the military forces of the Crown, their principal role being to raise and lead the local militia units which were formed for particular purposes, such as the suppression of local rebellions or when invasions by Scotland or France might be expected. Deputy Lieutenants are commissioned by the Lord Lieutenant and their role is to assist in the performance of any public duty performed by the Lord-Lieutenant. There is complicated formula for calculating the entitlement of DLs which is determined by the population of the County; for Somerset it is 51, but the number actually in post at the time of writing is 30 and I understand most counties do not take up their full entitlement. The Lord-Lieutenant may appoint a Vice Lord-Lieutenant from amongst the Deputies.

When I was appointed I realised that there were several soldiers and sailors who were DLs in Somerset, but that there were no airmen, so it looked as if I was filling an obvious gap. Walter Luttrell told me that most Lord-Lieutenants try personally to accept all the invitations they receive because, when people ask them to attend a function, they don't expect to see some unknown deputy turning up, so we tend to be asked to do something only when the Lord-Lieutenant is 'double booked'. In practice I only represented him once or twice a year, usually for functions with a military flavour or at memorial services. There is a uniform for Lord-Lieutenants and their Deputies, but military personnel may wear their own uniforms if they are of field rank (majors) or above. Lord-Lieutenants and DLs retire at the age of 75, or 10 years in post, whichever is later, but after retirement DLs are still entitled to use the letters 'DL'. There are no post nominal letters for a Lord-Lieutenant or Vice Lord-Lieutenant.

I asked a friend of mine who was a DL in another county what he did and he said that he spent most of his time going to the funerals of other deputies. Not a very onerous appointment, but one of which I have been extremely proud to have held.

Chapter 18

Reflections

Looking back over my life I can't help feeling that I have been incredibly lucky. I had a very happy childhood with my parents in Kent. I was able to take great pleasure and satisfaction in my chosen career and, above all, I have been happily married for over half a century with the joy of a wonderful family. What more can anyone ask? I was discussing my good fortune with a friend some time ago and he said, 'You know, John, we make our own luck'. I have often thought about this and I suppose to some extent it is true in that we can take advantage of opportunities presented to us, or even create those opportunities. But there must still be an element of luck in being in the right place at the right time. How different my life would have been if I hadn't taken my parents for a drink in a pub and met a complete stranger who introduced me to my future wife. How different it would have been if that wing commander had not allowed me to join his Mosquito Night Fighter course, just after I was commissioned, without any authority from above and while I was still officially on leave from a different Command. Furthermore, there have been incidents in my life which I have found difficult to explain as mere coincidences – perhaps those guardian angels really do exist.

From the day I was first taken up in that open-cockpit biplane seventy years ago I have always wanted to fly. As a teenager at school during the War I therefore naturally thought in terms of joining the Royal Air Force as soon as I could, but there were many potential hurdles to be negotiated, not least that of being able to pass the stringent medical tests.

I count myself very fortunate that I was among the last of those military pilots to learn to fly in an open- cockpit biplane with no radios or sophisticated navigational aids and, best of all, no Air Traffic Control. And to think I have actually been paid for doing what I wanted to do. John Magee expressed it perfectly when he wrote: 'Oh! I have slipped the surly bonds of Earth and danced the skies with laughter-silvered wings'. We must all have admired the beauty of the skies, especially when seen from an aircraft – not a day goes by when I don't look up and wonder at the scene. The skies are always changing, never the same, and always beautiful. They are very much part of the 'joy of flying' and that is what I originally wanted to call this book until Mr Google told me that at least seven other people had used the same title. While I have placed much emphasis on enjoying my chosen career, I honestly believe that, at the same time, we were doing a valuable job in helping to keep the peace.

I sometimes wish I had been born some ten years earlier because I would have loved to have been in the RAF in the formative years of the 1930s, flying those wonderful biplanes like the Hawker Fury or Gloster Gladiator. I would also have liked to have been old enough to have flown in the Battle of Britain, but maybe had I done that I might not have been around now to be able to pen these thoughts. I did however serve at a very interesting period of history in that I witnessed the effects of the Cold War at the sharp end. Not long after the Berlin Wall came down we went on a river cruise in 1995 from Moscow to St Petersberg. I found it an eerie experience to wander round the Kremlin taking photographs with no one taking any notice. Times certainly change.

For a short time I played with the idea of becoming an airline pilot, but I soon realized that I would be bored stiff with that type of flying – my passengers would certainly not have enjoyed aerobatics. The RAF on the other hand offered me a very satisfying career with plenty of variety, not only in the different aircraft I was able to fly, but also in a wide range of interesting jobs. I was not particularly ambitious as far as promotion was concerned because I was usually enjoying my current work too much to be thinking of anything else. When promotion came along I was just pleasantly surprised and I found that I then appreciated the extra responsibilities that accompanied the new job.

Although I have been flying for most of my working life I have only accumulated just under 4,000 hours in my log book which is not very much for a professional pilot. The reason for this is that most of my flying was carried out in short-endurance aircraft when sometimes one started to get short of fuel after forty minutes or so. On the other hand I have been able to fly a wide variety of aircraft types, operating in several different and interesting operational roles. I have also thoroughly enjoyed the chance of taking part in some exciting civil sporting aviation, thanks mainly to the Tiger Club.

When I started flying in the mid 1940s many different new aircraft were regularly being produced and the Society of British Aircraft Constructors' (SBAC) shows at Farnborough soon after the War were exciting events when test pilots did their best to show off their new mounts. Squadrons were re-equipping with new aircraft at relatively frequent intervals, but nowadays an aircraft might stay in operational service for forty or even fifty years like the Canberra and Hunter.

I joined my first squadron at a time when it was common practice for RAF pilots to change roles fairly frequently. However, the current full cost of training a pilot to 'wings' standard is about £1.25m and a further £50,000 for each subsequent hour on a Tornado. It is therefore obviously far more economic to stay in the same role for as long as possible. Furthermore since aircraft nowadays often stay in service for many years, pilots tend to continue on the same type for most of their flying careers. Thus it is now perfectly possible for a newly graduated pilot to have joined, say, a Typhoon squadron and then to finish up twenty years later as a group captain station commander on the same type. All of which means that it would be difficult for a young pilot these days to have the chance of flying and operating as many different aircraft as I have had the good fortune to do. The list of aircraft at Appendix 2 speaks for itself. As I have previously written, I have always thought that flying those wonderful wartime classics, such as the Lancaster and Spitfire on the CFS course early in my career, did more for my flying than a similar number of hours on the same type – which has been my excuse for trying to fly a new type whenever the opportunity occurred. But I must be honest when I say that I suspect my main motivation was because it was fun.

It is also expensive to post people around unnecessarily. We used to be posted every two years or so which is why we are now in our 26th home. Unless it is necessary to move someone for the benefit of their career, or for any other good reason, the current tendency is for people to be allowed to stay put for longer periods. It is now quite common for RAF personnel to stay in one post for ten years or more, which I would have found very tedious because I enjoyed the frequent new challenges and changes of scene. Curiously enough so did my wife, but then she knew what she was taking on when she married me. In fact sometimes we both used to get itchy feet after eighteen months or so.

One of the rewarding aspects of flying is that one is always learning. Many years ago I remember thinking that I learnt something new on every flight and that realization stayed with me throughout my career. In fact it can be positively dangerous to become complacent or overconfident in the air, as was demonstrated to me by several incidents which I have described in earlier chapters. Most pilots prefer flying in good weather rather than bad, but I found I used to enjoy the challenge of flying in bad weather, particularly when it was really bad; perhaps that is just my perverse nature showing itself.

I firmly believe that you can't do anything really well in this life unless you enjoy it. I have therefore always tried to ensure that pilots under my command have enjoyed their work. This in no way conflicts with the need to exercise strict flying discipline whether flying a multi–million pound military operational aircraft, a huge airliner with 500 passengers or a light civil type enjoying a local trip on a nice sunny day. We used to be told there were old pilots and bold pilots, but no old bold pilots.

I have been much impressed by reading about the way today's aircrews of all three services have coped with some of the very exacting and frightening operational sorties they have carried out during recent conflicts. I am also conscious of the fact that I have never flown in a hostile situation and I often wonder whether I would have coped as well. I will never know – I just hope that I would not have let the side down.

There are far fewer flying stations in the RAF than when I was serving. This has greatly reduced the opportunities for wing commanders and group captains to be given flying jobs – consequently once a wing commander has commanded a squadron he may think he will never get another flying appointment and therefore decides to leave the service to become an airline pilot. Some also leave at that stage simply to get more money. We lose many good people for these reasons. I count myself lucky in that I was able to continue flying throughout most of my forty-three years in uniform. I also think I was very fortunate to have spent only nine months in the Ministry during that time.

When we were first married it was unusual for officers' wives to go out to work unless they were professionals, such as doctors or lawyers. But these days, quite apart from the obvious economic advantages of doing so, most young wives seem to want to work, families permitting. If they have a good job perhaps they would prefer not to move around more than necessary. Deciding how best to educate one's children can be a problem. Relatively generous allowances help with paying boarding school fees and this allows children to have a stable education while parents move around the world, but this does not suit all families. Some families prefer to have a settled home with the wage-earner commuting home at weekends. We were forced to do this for about six months when I was on a course and I did not enjoy it.

There have been many changes in recent years which have affected the quality of life since I left the service. For example, in my time there were many exciting opportunities to serve overseas together with our families, but these days accompanied posts abroad are few and far between. Servicemen and women may now be required to serve abroad in operational theatres for extended periods, but without their families. We used to be given railway warrants when we went on leave, but that privilege has been withdrawn; admittedly some people might have taken advantage of the system and taken a holiday in the Shetlands rather than Exmoor, but it is an example of the things that made service life attractive being withdrawn. .

When we were first married very few RAF officers owned their own houses and not many married quarters were available, nevertheless we were usually able to rent houses locally. Our first cottage was a tiny one up and one down and was, in fact, called 'But an' Ben'. Money was tight and the luxuries which young married couples now seem to take for granted were simply not available –

neither did we expect them – but we were very happy and still managed to have a lot of fun. The rapidly increasing house prices of the 1970s changed things in that most RAF families felt they had to get on the ladder and invest in bricks and mortar. This has had a dramatic effect on station life because house owners would naturally want to rush off home at the end of a day's work, whereas previously they and their wives might have taken part in activities on the station.

One of the biggest changes has been the massive move towards putting work – normally carried out by serving personnel – out to civil contractors. For instance, much of the servicing of aircraft is now carried out by civilian engineers, and catering has also been civilianized on many stations, resulting in the cost of functions increasing due to the higher costs of using civilian staff. Civilianization may or may not have saved public money, but few people I have spoken to think these are changes for the better. One of the spin-offs from this policy has been that some stations have found it more difficult to find sufficient service personnel to carry out all those extra jobs that need to be done, like guard duties, or even finding sufficient people to produce good sporting teams. This can put an extra load on servicemen and women resulting in some cases with a lowering of morale. Those of us who are privileged enough to be able to fly aeroplanes must never forget that our good fortune is only made possible by the dedication and skill of those who maintain and service our mounts. Our lives are, quite literally, in their hands. The relationship between RAF pilots and the servicemen and women who looked after us was invariable close; but is this still the case with civil engineers?

We used to have big station parades every Saturday morning which would start with prayers being read by the Church of England padre. But before the prayers the parade commander – usually the station commander – would order, 'Fall out the Roman Catholics and Jews'. They would then march to the edge of the parade ground, face outwards, and wait to be called back after the prayers. Just imagine the outcry if we tried to introduce such a procedure which now seems archaic, even comic. Since the advent of the five-day week such parades are only held on very special occasions, but, I hasten to add, without the exclusions.

Commanding officers these days have to manage their own budgets. This obviously makes them all much more cost conscious, which is a good thing, but I'm glad I didn't have to do it. At least commanders are now aware of financial considerations when making decisions, whereas in my day, if I tried to find out how much something was going to cost, the information was simply not available. Unfortunately along with the budgets has come the introduction of American-style business speak. We have mission statements and agencies (whatever they are), and I can't help feeling that sometimes we are tending to replace leadership with management. I went to a briefing recently for retired senior officers and we had a talk from an air vice-marshal in the Ministry of

My 70th birthday present from my three daughters – 10 laps round the Castle Combe Circuit.
John L E Gaisford

Defence. His talk was so full of buzzwords that I could not understand much of what he was trying to say – and I wasn't the only one in the audience who felt like that.

We are thoroughly enjoying retirement although I find myself becoming rather busier than I would have wished. But that is my own fault because I have found it difficult to say 'no' when asked to do something locally. From my point of view both my seventieth and eightieth birthdays were highlights. For the former my three daughters gave me a surprise present of a one–day advanced driving course in a racing car at the Castle Combe circuit. Not only was this most exciting and thoroughly enjoyable, but I also learnt a lot about my own driving. I had always admired racing drivers for being able to handle their cars at high speed when only a few feet away from each other, but I found that I had to concentrate so hard just to drive the car properly that I could not possibly have coped with having to deal with other cars around me. I now watch Formula One with even more admiration than I did before.

As a pilot, I have always admired birds because they can fly so much better than we can. You seldom see a bird do a bad landing and I have yet to see a mid-air collision, even though they sometimes fly very close together in huge flocks. It was therefore a very pleasant surprise when I was treated to a visit to a falconry centre for my eightieth birthday. We spent the morning learning about the birds and then flying them; watching a big bird such as an eagle owl coming towards you and then landing accurately on one's fist was very thrilling. Finally we even went hunting in the afternoon, but without success. Nevertheless it was fascinating to watch the hawk working with its falconer.

Birds do it better! An 80th birthday present with 'Yarak Birds of Prey'.

I think it is fashionable to say 'Things were not like that in my day', and I suppose all previous generations have said the same thing. I only hope that today's servicemen and women get as much satisfaction, and dare I say it, fun, out of life as we did.

For the past few years I had harboured the secret wish to celebrate my eightieth birthday by flying in a Tiger Moth. I had not flown one for forty years and I wanted to test the bicycle theory – 'once you can ride a bike you can always ride a bike.' Charlie Shea-Simonds made this possible for me by letting me fly with him from Netheravon in the beautiful aircraft which he had restored himself. I was delighted to find that the bicycle theory worked and that I was still able to

1935.   *2005.*

fly a light aircraft reasonably respectably. After I touched down on my first landing Charlie said, 'Now go round again and prove to me that wasn't a fluke!' The day was made even more nostalgic because my old friend John Urmston, who lived not far away and was a friend of Charlie's, also flew with him just after me. It was a wonderful experience for us both and, as you can well imagine, we all celebrated our delightful reunion with the sky that evening.

I have often been asked what my favourite aircraft was and I have always said that it was an extremely difficult question to answer because there were so many of them. My first love was, of course, the Tiger Moth, but many others such as the Mosquito, Spitfire, Hornet, Meteor, Venom, Hunter, Gazelle and Lightning, not forgetting the little Turbulent, came very close seconds. But the winner has to be ... the Tiger Moth.

Appendix 1
Record of Service

The Principal appointments are listed in bold type:

Sep 1940–Dec 1941	Marlborough College Officers' Training Corps	Private
Jan 1942–Aug 1943	No. 529 (Marlborough Schools) Squadron ATC	Corporal
Sep 1942–Jul 1943	Marlborough College Home Guard	Private
Oct 1943–Apr 1944	Cambridge University Air Squadron	
Apr 1944–Jun 1944	No. 6 Air Crew Reception Centre, Scarborough	Cadet
Jun 1944–Jul 1944	**No. 4 Elementary Flying Training School, Brough** *(Tiger Moth)*	
Aug 1944	Aircrew Dispatch Centre, Heaton Park	
Aug 1944–Sep 1944	No. 8 School of Technical Training, Blackpool	
Sep 1944–Dec 1944	HQ No. 75 Signals Wing, Broadstairs	
Dec 1944–Jan 1945	Aircrew Dispatch Centre, Heaton Park	
Jan 1945–Feb 1945	Air Crew Officers' School, Hereford	
Feb 1945–May 1945	**No. 11 Elementary Flying Training School, Perth** *(Tiger Moth)*	
May 1945–Oct 1945	**No. 19 Flying Training School, Cranwell** *(Harvard)*	
Nov 1945–Dec 1945	Air Crew Officers' School, Hereford	Pilot Officer
Jan 1946–Mar 1946	No. 17 Air Crew Holding Unit, Snaith	
Mar 1946–May 1946	No. 54 Operational Training Unit, East Moor *(Mosquito)*	
May 1946–Jul 1946	**No. 264 Night Fighter Squadron, Church Fenton,** *(Mosquito)*	
Jul 1946–April 1947	**No. 264 Squadron, Linton-on-Ouse** *(Mosquito)*	Flying Officer
Apr 1947–Jan 1948	**No. 264 Squadron, Wittering** *(Mosquito)*	
Jan 1948	**No. 264 Squadron, Coltishall** *(Mosquito)*	
Jan 1948–July 1948	**Central Flying School, Little Rissington** *(Various Types)*	
Jul 1948–Aug 1950	**RAF College, Cranwell** *(Prentice and Harvard)*	Flight Lieutenant
Aug 1950–Oct 1953	**Central Flying School, Staff Instructor & P.A. to the Comdt**	
Oct 1953–Dec 1953	**No. 229 (Fighter) Operational Conversion Unit,** Chivenor *(Vampire)*	
Jan 1954–May 1955	**No. 98 (Day Fighter/Ground Attack) Squadron, Fassberg** *(Venom)* **(AFC)**	*Flight Cdr*
Mar 1955–May 1955	Day Fighter Leaders School, West Raynham *(Hunter)*	
May 1955–Jan 1956	**No. 98 (DF/GA) Squadron, Jever** *(Hunter)*	
Jan 1956–Sep 1957	**No. 26 (DF/GA) Squadron, Oldenburg** *(Hunter)*	Sqdn Leader
Oct 1957–Jul 1958	Air Ministry, Air Secretary's Department	*Sqdn Cdr*
Nov 1957	No. 231 Operational Conversion Unit, Bassingbourn *(Canberra)*	

Jul 1958–Dec 1961	Equerry to HRH The Duke of Edinburgh (LVO)	
Jan 1962–Dec 1962	RAF Staff College, Bracknell	Wing Cdr
Jan 1963–Feb 1963	School of Refresher Flying, Manby, *(Meteor)*	
Dec 1962–Apr 1964	RAF Middleton St George *(Javelin & Lightning)*	OC Flying Wing
Apr 1964–Jun 1965	No. 226 Operational Conversion Unit, Coltishall *(Lightning)*	Chief Instructor
Jun 1965–Dec 1965	Joint Services Staff College, Latimer	
Jan 1966–Nov 1967	HQ Middle East Command, Aden, Operations Staff (OBE)	
Feb 1968–Jun 1968	Joint Services Staff College, Latimer, Directing Staff	
Jun 1968–Aug 1970	HQ Strike Command, Bentley Priory, Group Captain Organisation	Group Captain
Aug 1970–Sep 1970	School of Refresher Flying, Manby *(Jet Provost)*	
Oct 1970–Jan 1971	No. 236 Operational Conversion Unit, St Mawgan *(Nimrod)*	
Jan 1971–Dec 1972	RAF Kinloss *(Nimrod)*	Station Cdr
Jan 1973–Dec 1973	Royal College of Defence Studies, Seaford House	
Dec 1973–Jan 1974	No. 3 Flying Training School, Leeming *(Jet Provost)*	Air Commodore
Jan 1974	No. 4 Flying Training School, Valley *(Gnat)*	
Feb 1974–Feb 1976	Central Flying School, Little Rissington *(Various Training Types)*	Commandant
Feb 1976–Feb 1978	HQ Training Command, Brampton, Air Commodore Flying Training	
Mar 1978–May 1980	HQ Southern Maritime Air Region, Mount Batten	Air Vice-Marshal
Aug 1980–Jan 1982	Retirement Mk 1, Somerset	Air Commander
Jan 1982–Jan 1989	The Queen's Flight, Benson (KCVO)	
Jan 1989–?	Retirement Mk 2, Somerset (DL)	Captain

Appendix 2
Aircraft Flown

1st Pilot Military	1st Pilot Civil	1st Pilot Gliders	Aircraft handled but not as 1st Pilot	
			Military	*Civil*
Tiger Moth	Auster Mk 4	Schule	Lincoln	Tristar 500
Harvard Mk 2b	Auster Aiglet	Primary Glider	Halifax Mk 8	Dakota
Mosquito Mks 3, 6, 29,	Auster Autocrat	T 21	Valetta	KZ VII (Denmark)
30, & 36	Auster Airdale	Cadet 2	Varsity	Cherokee
Lancaster Mk 3	Cygnet	Prefect	Martinet Siebel	Baron
Hornet Mk 1	Vega Gull	Grunau	Wellington	Cessna 180 Floatplane
Auster Mks 4, 5, 6, & 7	Tipsy B	MU 13	Heron	Miles Student M100
Master Mk 2	Tipsy Nipper		Beverley (Aden)	Zlin 526
Martinet Mk1	Fairey Junior		Twin Pioneer (Aden)	Pitts 2a
Prentice Mk 1	Taylor Monoplane		Argosy	Duet
Piston Provost	Turbulent		Hastings T5	PA 28
Jet Provost Mks 3, 4, & 5	Jodel D117		Belfast	Fuji FA200
Chipmunk Mk 10	Turbi-Sport		Hercules	Musketeer
Balliol Mks 1 & 2	Active Mk 2		Andover Mk2	Cherokee
Athena Mk 2	Hornet Moth		BAe 146	Cessna 172
Oxford Mk 1	Puss Moth		Islander	Shrike Commander
Anson Mks 1, 12, 19 & 21	Jackaroo		CF5 (Canada)	Turbo Commander
Devon	Currie Wot,		T39 (USA)	Navaho
Gnat Mk 1	Hot Wot		SAAB 105 (Sweden)	Safir (Sweden)
Bulldog	Wizz Wot		Draken (Sweden)	Supermunk
Cessna T 37 (Jordan)	Garland Linnet		Jaguar T2	Bf 108 Taifun
Spitfire Mk XVI	Comper Swift		F 104b (Jordan)	VFW 614
Vampire Mks 3, 5, & 11	Messenger		Jetstream	Seneca 1 & 2
Venom Mks 1 & 4	Prospector		Beaver	Dornier Do 28
Meteor Mks 4, 7, 8 & 12	B.A. Swallow		Dominie	Meta Sokol
Sea Fury Mk 20	Super Cub 95, 150		Sea Prince	Fokker F27
Hunter Mks 1, 4, 6, 7,	Tri-Pacer		AN12 (India)	DH Dash 7 (Canada)
& 7a	Aztec		Sikorsky R4	Vertol 107
Sabre Mk 4	Comanche		S76 (Jordan)	Jet Ranger
Javelin Mk 3	Cessna 150		Alouette 2 (Jordan)	
Lightning Mks 1, !a, 2,	Cessna 182		Sycamore	
3, 4 & 5	Cessna 210		Skeeter	
Canberra Mks 2, 4 & 6	Cessna 310		Scout (Aden)	
Gannet Mk 2	Robin HR 200		Huey (Canada)	
Nimrod Mk1	Sundowner		Kiowa (Canada)	
Shackleton MR 2,	Airtourer		Puma	
Dragonfly	Ambassadeur		Sea King	
Sioux	Mascaret		Lynx	
Whirlwind Mk 10	Stampe		Wessex Mk4	
Gazelle	Rallye		Black Hawk	
	Aircoupe			
	Pup 100			
	Wallis Gyroplane			

Index